Constance Roy
173 Lisbon St.
Lewiston
Maine.

THE STORY OF

Orchestral Music

and Its Times

THE STORY OF
Orchestral Music and Its Times

*

by

PAUL GRABBE

Drawings by John C. Wonsetler

GROSSET & DUNLAP

Publishers   NEW YORK

To the memory of

Alexander Grosset

who asked me to do this book
ten years ago.

CONTENTS

Contents

NOTE: Composers treated in this book are distinguished in the index by being set in capital letters.

MUSIC IN THE STREAM OF HISTORY

Describing the music of his times, Thomas Morley, famous English composer of madrigals, wrote in the year 1597: *"The pavane is a kind of staide musicke ordained for grave dauncing."*

This sentence is revealing. It places Morley in time and space, for it conveys the flavor of another age, the implications of another kind of life. In listening to Morley's music, we are, in the same way, at once projected back into the long ago. However much this music may delight us, it obviously is not expressive of our times. It mirrors the character and spirit of Merrie England under Elizabeth—a period when in every parish people foregathered after supper to sing madrigals; when the ability to read at sight these fresh and tuneful three or four part songs was so common that almost everyone of

[1]

culture and refinement joined in this favorite pastime.

This widespread craving for song is part of a whole way of life. In time it disappears. Another century is here imposing social change and readjustment. A different outlook and a different way of life are brought with each succeeding century. And in each age the spirit of the times is reflected in all art. As H. Van Buren Magonigle has said:

"Art is integral with the fabric of life. It is not a separate stream running parallel with the current of human events. It is one of the threads of that current, and the sweep of life and the progress of art are identical in movement."

This integration can be clearly traced in music. Not all composers are equally affected by the trends and currents of the world in which they live. Some speak the language of the past, some of the present, and some anticipate the future. But on the whole the course of music is affected, and for this reason it is helpful to see it in relation to its times.

The music which we hear today covers a period of, roughly, 350 years. It dates from the time when a momentous shift in music became apparent. Conveniently historians take the year 1600 as marking the new trend.

In the preceding age the instruments in use

were still unstandardized and crude, and music meant the human voice. The art of song had reached a high peak of development, and choirs sang religious works, almost, if not as complicated, as choral and orchestral music of today. Like some great tapestry of sound this choral music, with the exalted beauty of its weblike, interweaving melodies, seemed to envelop all the music genius of the Western world.

In the great madrigals, motets, and masses of Palestrina and di Lasso, and in the English madrigals of Byrd and Morley, choral music had attained a perfection never equalled before or since. This was its culminating point, the Golden Age of song.

And now a sudden flood of new ideas, new instruments, new genius—and social change—marks a transition from the religious to the secular and from the vocal to the instrumental. It is this shift that leads directly to the appearance of the orchestra, early in the 17th century, and to the subsequent emergence of the music we enjoy today.

THE SEVENTEENTH—

is an important, an exciting century in music. It is an age of promise, of emergence, boasting at least two figures of purest genius: Monteverdi in Italy, Purcell in England. It is a century made memorable by its bold searching, its adventuring, its breaking of new ground, not alone in music, but in every field. For, with the seventeenth century come the beginnings of the modern world; the passing of the medieval. It is an age of "firsts" in politics, in thought, in science, in economics.

For the first time those supreme arbiters of Europe's fate, the Pope and the Holy Roman Empire, yield to a new nationalism, to the defiance of Protestantism, to slowly widening oriental and colonial trade. The old feudal system is being left behind as Europe's numerous small vassal states are gradually bound together into larger units—units which take on the shape of ever stronger monarchy. In France Louis XIV becomes the first absolute monarch; the first king to overcome the power of the feudal lords, to conceive ruling as a profession, to assume total authority which strengthens the nation yet leads it into costly wars.

And wars are different now. The armies are no longer composed of levies, servants fighting at the command of feudal masters. They are mercenaries, and they demand their pay. So war is more expensive, and more professional, and, with plundering and marauding mercenaries, more devastating.

Over in England the Stuart King tries to follow the European trend toward absolute rule by Divine Right. But the rising English bourgeoisie won't have it. Parliament brings the King to trial—and executes him. All Europe, and even England itself, is shocked by the precedent. Never has there been such sacrilege, such defiance of the natural order of things. New, too, in this adventure are the Ironsides who fight for Cromwell—an army of men rallied around a belief. Not levies, nor mercenaries, but free men fighting for a cause.

And the Dutch burghers, arming every available man and succeeding in defeating the mighty, seasoned, professional, armies of Spain; freeing themselves and setting up a republic. This is new!

[5]

Seventeenth Century

Newest of all is the land across the sea. A freer world is opening up, and whole families leave home to colonize the Atlantic coast from Maine to Carolina.

Suddenly in England we hear for the first time the thundering of the Voice of the People. Parliament, revolting once more from the reinstated Stuart kings, finally has done with Divine Right and wins her great Bill of Rights with William and Mary.

Side by side with all of this Newton is giving to the world the scientific method, the law of gravitation, deductive reasoning; Galileo is working with the new telescope, revealing the mysteries of the constellations. John Locke is proposing a society ordered according to natural law: man's right to life, liberty—and property. Defoe is creating the novel, the first literature of and for the common man, while Shakespeare in the drama, Descartes in philosophy, and Bacon and Hobbes and Milton are all launching new ideas—the roots of 18th and 19th century flowerings.

For the coming mastery of the sea could not be achieved without the compass and barometer. Science could hardly develop without the telescope and the microscope. Medicine could scarcely begin without quinine and the thermometer. All these come out of the age of great beginnings, the 17th century!

In music, too, this is a century of "firsts." For it is the age of the hoeing and the planting of the ground from which our modern art will spring. The first impulse for this new music comes from Italy.

It is in Florence that a group of "amateurs in all the arts"—Peri, Caccini, and others—foregather to discuss the art of classical antiquity. Although they seek merely to determine the way in which the Greeks used music in their drama, these Florentines quite inadvertently originate the opera. Into this new form Monteverdi breathes the spark of life. He injects into it both pathos and ardent passion—a far cry from music's beautiful, impersonal fluidity of but a generation back. His efforts are immediately successful. The newly invented *"dramma per musica"* catches on and sweeps all Europe. In 1637 Venice builds the first opera house. Soon London, Paris, Rome, and Hamburg follow suit. Before the century's half way mark is reached, an introduction to the opera—the overture—has been invented; the orchestra has come to life. It is no longer a haphazard gathering of different instrumentalists but an ensemble grouped in accordance with a predetermined plan.

This early orchestra, according to our standards, is small and crude. It lacks an underlying science for the differentiation of the instruments and their capacities. A keyboard instrument, usually a harpsichord, still takes the lead and fills in the bare spots. But it is a beginning. It is something new.

Paralleling these developments goes the improvement of existing instruments. The singing violin, invented in the previous century in Italy, spreads throughout Europe. (It will eventually supersede the popular viol, soft-spoken instrument of aristocracy.) The organ is so far perfected that Frescobaldi, Buxtehude and other great performers on the instrument have arisen. The age of virtuoso playing on the harpsichord as well as on the organ is at hand; and music suitable for star performance is in demand.

Instrumentalists, having practically no literature of their own, have so far been content with *playing* the madrigals. Soon they develop possibilities which human voices were unable to achieve. To fill the need for this different, *instrumental* music, composers string together folk dances of various nations, originating the dance suite. Other new forms emerge—the instrumental fugue, the fantasia, and the sonata. These are intended to be played instead of sung, and into the new instrumental music composers pour their best creative efforts. Thus fewer madrigals are written and the form begins to disappear.

[8]

Change is quite clearly in the air. The transition in music from the religious to the secular is everywhere in evidence. Hand in hand with it goes the gradual shift from the vocal to the instrumental. In England the process is speeded because of the outcries of the Puritans against organs and choral singing in the churches. Here is but one of many forces which now adds impetus to the development of secular instrumental music.

Concurrently with this development comes the growing popularity of the major and minor scales; the gradual relegation to the attic of the ecclesiastic modes; the dawn of modern harmony. Music gradually takes on a different complexion. Composers are no longer solely preoccupied with the creation of a pattern of interweaving melodies. They have become aware of the emotional intensity to be attained from a single melody projected on a background of chords.

All of these new materials make for an intensely stimulating period. They are portents of a new era which will bear fruit as soon as all the gains have been assimilated. This will occur in the next century, one of the greatest in the history of music.

JAMESTOWN, VA., SETTLED

OTHER EVENTS: Use of dining forks ("Italian neatnesses") spreads to England; Shakespeare's "Hamlet" in its 4th year. Henry Hudson sails to find trade route to China. Frenchmen read first book on etiquette. Russia faces years of chaos following abortive reign of Boris Godounov. Ravenscroft, English composer, finds and jots down "Three Blind Mice." Jesuits discover quinine in Peru. Cervantes' "Don Quixote" delights Spain. Monteverdi composes

ORFEO; OPERA IN 5 ACTS (SEE PAGE 195).

In the year 1600 a book appeared in Venice protesting vigorously against modernism in music and complaining particularly that the new generation of composers were interested mainly with "delighting sense and not with satisfying reason." The protest was aimed in part at Monteverdi, lean and harassed mastercomposer of madrigals, in the employ of the powerful Duke of Mantua.

This Italian nobleman, though cruel, had a

streak of generousness with which he favored his musicians, dogs, and lady loves alike. To celebrate the marriage of his son, he ordered Monteverdi to produce a piece for the theatre and to spare no expense.

It was for this festive occasion that Monteverdi wrote his *Orfeo,* which to this day remains a vitally expressive work of art. To realize his aim, Monteverdi assembled the players employed by the Duke: 15 viols, 2 violins, 4 flutes, 2 hautboys, 2 cornets, 4 trumpets, 4 trombones, 2 harpsichords, 2 little organs, a regal, a harp—and taught them to play together. *Orfeo,* however, marked merely a beginning. By 1627 Monteverdi had invented startling new effects, the tremolo and pizzicato; he had installed the violin as the backbone of his ensemble; had trained his players. And now the orchestra emerges as a coherent whole, still crude, but pulling together to realize the will of the composer.

JAPAN CLOSES DOOR TO WHITE MAN

OTHER EVENTS: To house remains of his favorite wife, India's Shah Jehan builds Taj Mahal. Dutch inhabitants of Manhattan Island erect 1st wooden church; few American settlers as yet enjoy the luxury of window panes. In France, Vincent de Paul, inspired charity worker, succors galley slaves; establishes 1st soup kitchens. With his improved telescope Galileo notes the phases of the moon. Cardinal Richelieu invents mayonnaise. Schütz composes . . .

3 GEISTLICHE CONZERTE (SEE PAGE 203).

Heinrich Schütz, called the "father of German music," came of a well-to-do Saxon family. He was well educated and became in time an organist, conductor, and composer.

When Schütz was forty-two, the King of Saxony, to celebrate the marriage of his daughter, the Princess Sophie, decided to import from Italy Peri's *Dafne*, one of those novel "dramas set to music" about which so much had recently been heard. When *Dafne* was translated into

German, it was discovered that the music no longer fitted the words of the libretto. To remedy this situation the King decided to have the music re-worked by a native composer. Schütz got the job, and thus became known to posterity as the founder of German opera.

These labors, however, were incidental, for his main contributions lay in religious music. In this field he pioneered, introducing such innovations as double choirs and instrumental accompaniment, thus bridging the gap between his great predecessor, Palestrina, and his great successor, Bach. From Italy Schütz borrowed the new dramatic style, which he adapted to the more sober requirements of the church. His *Three Spiritual Concerts* illustrate this mood of "dramatic reverence." These works are quite remarkable for their frequent directions in the score, specifying how the music is to be performed—a practice at that time still virtually unknown.

FRANCE
EVOLVES
COAT AND VEST

OTHER EVENTS: Blind Milton dictates last page of "Paradise Lost." "Curious brew," Englishmen say but drink with relish tea newly introduced from China. Isaac Newton's law of gravity startles scientists. Habeas Corpus Act passes Br. Parliament. In Italy, Antonio Stradivari produces 1st signed instrument; society still scorns violin except for the dance. Connecticut Code of Law still grants parents life and death power over offspring. Lully composes . . .

THESÉE; OPERA IN FIVE ACTS (SEE PAGE 194).

"He had a clever but vulgar face," writes Romain Rolland, "and heaving eyebrows." He was inordinately ambitious; he understood the all-powerfulness of money; and he advanced his fortunes through every form of low and sordid business intrigue. "With it all, he was a great musician."

Lully was Italian born, the son of a Florentine miller. At fourteen, knowing no music but playing the guitar, he came to France. Before

[14]

long he had become a renowned violinist; then a composer, a favorite at the court of Louis XIV; then virtually the musical dictator of all France. In time he became thoroughly French.

Lully wrote much music, trained musicians, supervised performances. He was indefatigable, and through it all he remained the shrewd observer. Noting the Frenchman's fondness for the dance and his dislike of noisy passion, Lully toned down Italian opera and mixed it with the elegance of French ballet, thus laying the foundation of French opera. He also developed the overture, as in *Thesée,* which marks one of the first appearances in the orchestra of the kettledrums. Lully was especially at his ease in compositions conveying the noble dignity and soothing tenderness of pastoral emotion. Ironically, he died of blood poisoning after injuring his leg with a heavy conductor's rod with which he thumped the floor while leading the orchestra.

1665-84

LLOYD'S STARTS IN COFFEE HOUSE

OTHER EVENTS: J. C. Denner of Nuremberg invents the clarinet. Founding of Bank of England takes banking away from goldsmiths. At Versailles, Louis XIVth holds Continent's most brilliant court; fountains and waterworks are Europe's wonder. Br. Parliament passes Bill of Rights. Massachusetts offers bounties for Indian scalps. Voltaire born. Men carry muffs; wear periwigs and lace cravats. Psychology acquires modern meaning. Purcell composes . . .

DIDO AND AENEAS; OPERA (SEE PAGE 197).

Henry Purcell came of a long line of English musicians, stretching back 150 years. Being immensely gifted and following in the footsteps of his father and his uncle, he started early collecting musical court jobs. For since the King was in the habit of keeping his musicians waiting for their pay, a musician's chances to make a living were considered greater if he could hold several appointments and claim back pay for each.

[16]

In addition to his more serious compositions, Purcell, in his capacity of court composer, turned out a quantity of trifling birthday odes and welcome songs; but all of these he tossed off with what has been described as "reckless mastery," for he was extraordinarily precocious and prolific.

The orchestra for which Purcell composed was still primitive. It had no French horns, as yet no clarinets, and Purcell could not depend on good performance even from the strings since violins had only recently been introduced in England. Nevertheless he put this orchestra to splendid use, producing works that are distinguished by their freshness, subtlety, variety, and rich poetic power. Toward the end of his career Purcell turned his attention to theatrical music. *Dido and Aeneas*, his only opera, composed for performance at a girls' boarding school, is delightful music, rated as one of Purcell's most outstanding works.

1689-94

THE EIGHTEENTH—

As this century opens there is in progress in London a Masked Ball where dashing cavaliers and their ladies, resplendent in costumes of satin and velvet, laugh and dance through palatial halls. In Vienna, at the Royal Palace, an opera with its throng of performers, its gorgeous, magically moved scenic effects, brings gasps of pleasure from Emperor Charles and his courtiers. At the palace of Louis XIV of France a ballet of exquisite grace is staged. At the castle of the powerful Prince of Esterhazy, a talented Kapellmeister leads a splendid orchestra.

The keynote of the times is splendor and magnificence, and these are richly interwoven with refinement and elegance in all the multitude of courts, in all the capitals of Europe.

Each court is the throbbing heart of an empire, a kingdom, or a duchy. For the monarchic age is in full swing and Europe is parceled out in family properties. Austria and its horde of dependencies belongs to the Hapsburgs; France and Spain and their dependent kingdoms and duchies to the Bourbons; Prussia to the Hohenzollerns. There is besides a whole patchwork of smaller states—and all are subject to the rights of inheritance, the vagaries of intrigue, the conquests of war. The Ruling Families are for the most part benevolent despots, trying to hold in check a swarm of reactionary, feudal-minded nobles. The peasant mass groans under the weight of supporting this costly superstructure. Today their heavy taxes are paid to Austria, tomorrow to Spain. What does it matter? The taxes remain the same.

Yet this is to be the Age of Reason, the dawn of liberal thought and rationalism pushing through to republicanism—even to a glance ahead to democracy. How shall this be?

How shall John Locke's ideas of a Reasoned Order proposing government by consent of the governed fight its way through the accepted rule of privilege? Fight its way through in spite of a constant procession of costly, exhausting wars?

All Europe is scrambling over whether a Hapsburg or a Bourbon is to sit on the Spanish throne; how much of her vast inheritance it would be safe to allow to accrue to Maria Theresa of Austria. At the same time England and France are fighting a Seven Years War on land, at sea, and over the seas, for colonies and empire. Where does reason come in?

Somewhere between the struggles of dynasties at the top and the miseries of the poor beneath, scientists are at work. Dr. Jenner is discovering vaccination. Lavoisier is introducing chemistry. Diderot and other French encyclopedists are gathering and classifying existing knowledge for all the world to read. Inventors are launching the Industrial Revolution with the spinning jenny and the steam engine. Agriculture is taking a new turn with planting in furrows and the rotation of crops; and far-flung colonies are expanding trade by leaps and bounds. There are fortunes to be made in shipping around the world and in goods to be bought and sold. Centers of trade are becoming thriving cities; cities are building factories, and the peasantry is moving in. Wage earning has begun.

And through it all in increasing volume we hear the voices of John Locke, apostle of the middle class in politics, and Adam Smith, apostle of the middle class in economics, asserting the rights of the people in government and in free enterprise. And now Voltaire takes up the cry of liberalism with so brilliantly sharp a pen, the despots themselves are converts.

Upon this scene bursts the American Revolution. The cry of freedom rings around the world. Unperturbed, the crowned heads of

Europe see only England's loss of Empire. But the American blaze has crossed the ocean. France is in revolt. "Liberty, Equality, Fraternity," the people cry. And Louis XVI and Marie Antoinette go to Madame Guillotine.

Now the crowned heads are alarmed. "Stop it! Stop this horror!" they all shout. Powerful old Austria shouts it; the new Prussia, made great and military and reformed by Frederick the Great echoes the cry. "Stop them!" shouts Britain, grown rich through far-flung trade and rapid industrialization, and become through her wars, Mistress of the High Seas. Only the mighty voice of Russia, the new European power risen through the ruthless Westernizing of Peter the Great, is silent. Silent because the half crazy tyrant, Paul, sits on its throne.

Such is the European scene during one of the greatest centuries in music.

This music is an accurate reflection of the age. At first the temper of the times is one of breadth, magnificence, and great vitality. This is mirrored in the elaborateness and splendor of Italian opera, in the exuberant yet easy-flowing forcefulness of Händel, and in the sweep and grandeur of Johann Sebastian Bach. After the century's half-way mark is reached a different mood appears, and in the music of the times we note the change. Mozart, Haydn and other composers of the period reflect a society which has embarked upon an Age of Reason with order, clarity, precision as its chief ideals; an age, too, when court life has become sated with luxurious display and has turned to elegance, refinement, and sophistication.

During the early decades of the century, Italy is the center of all operatic life. Here is the mecca to which musicians travel by the hundreds to learn their art. From Italy they radiate in all directions, picking off the best plums in patronage and court appointments; for all of Europe's capitals have swallowed this Italian music whole. Spain, England, Russia are, operatically speaking, Italian colonies. Even Berlin is an outpost of Rome, though the Italians do not hold Germany in high esteem. It is a country, writes a Venetian chronicler in 1750 "not likely to produce musical genius." A people given to shouting when they sing.

Empty words, these, for the supremacy of the Italians is already slipping. Their *"dramma per musica,"* given such an auspicious start by Monteverdi, has sunk to a low level. What the Italians now applaud is vocal pyrotechnics; what dazzles them is tinsel in stage settings. Already the true center of operatic art is shifting elsewhere. Ironically, it will be the German, Gluck, producing in Paris, who will come forward to clean their house; to reinstate dramatic truth, thus taking opera back to the intentions of its founders.

But opera is only one aspect of the musical vitality in this prolific age. In another field composers are laboring in relative obscurity. They are perfecting instrumental music, and it is mainly their efforts that will be remembered later on.

To understand this other side of music it is important to remember that in the 18th century non-operatic music exists chiefly by the grace of wealthy noblemen, each with his princely court and court musicians. To maintain a small orchestra, to hire a composer (and possibly to dress him up in livery) is to the musically minded nobleman a necessary part of graceful living. The better the orchestra, the finer the composer, the greater the prestige.

Even the most vital creative spirits of the age —Bach and Handel, Mozart and Haydn, Corelli and Scarlatti and Rameau—are dependent on the generous but often petty and tyrannical bounty of these powerful princes, dukes, and archbishops. Serving these masters, composers must conform to princely taste. In the first half of the century they must be boldly picturesque, express a massive luxuriance touching the epic; in the second, they must adopt a style that is lighthearted but not frivolous, intelligent yet not too deep. Their music must be clear, symmetrical, well-mannered. It must embody the spirit which later generations will describe as Classicism. Strict etiquette must be observed in music no less than in dress and manners, and all expression of strong feeling is officially taboo.

In spite of these restrictions the genius of this age is such that music moves forward by giant strides. This is especially apparent in the progress of music for the orchestra.

During this period the orchestra is gradually expanded and refined. In Bach's time, early in the century, it is still small, comprising some twenty or twenty-five players. Of these a few, usually violinists, are soloists who play almost continuously, while the main body of performers joins in from time to time, for emphasis and volume. In Haydn's time, fifty years later, a transformation has occurred. Now the orchestra is broken up into four sections—strings, woodwinds, brass, percussion—and in this scheme the harpsichord, formerly the central pivot of the orchestra, drops out. Composers have come to realize that strings can be employed alone or blended with woodwinds, or that the latter can be used with brass; and that the blending of these groups for contrast and variety is opening up a new world of tonal possibilities.

The emergence of this richer conception of

the orchestra goes hand in hand with the development of a more complex structural pattern in orchestral music—the symphony. At first this is a super overture comprising three contrasted movements—quick, slow, quick. These movements may be animated, sad, dance-like, or meditative, but they remain light entertainment. Only in the hands of Mozart and Haydn, towards the ends of their careers, does the new form begin to show its powers in the expression of real force and deep emotion. It is at this point that instrumental music may be said to have come of age.

And now the stage is set for a revolutionary genius to appear and forge music into a universal language. Indeed he has appeared. As the century closes, Beethoven, a child of the Revolutionary Age, is nearing thirty. He is already a composer, and his music has already transcended its times, uniting the characteristics of the 18th and 19th centuries and pointing the way toward Romanticism.

MASS EMIGRATION
OF GERMANS
TO AMERICA

OTHER EVENTS: Peter the Great turns swamp into St. Petersburg, Russia's "window to Europe." Together with Dutch forces British besiege and seize Gibraltar. Handel's trumpeter invents the tuning fork. Italian, Christofori, constructs first piano. In Saxony, alchemist Bötgen is ordered by the King to turn base metal into gold; produces Europe's 1st hard porcelain. Scotland unites with England. Slave riots in New York suppressed. Corelli composes

CONCERTO GROSSO IN G MINOR; "CHRISTMAS" CONCERTO, OP. 6, NO. 8 (SEE PAGE 182).

Italians called him *"Il virtuosissimo di violino"* and kings and princes sought his company, but his contemporaries attest that he remained modest and amiable and very simple in dress and habits.

Corelli was the first outstanding master of the violin, a great teacher and composer as well as a great player. He made the violin respectable by supplying performers with something to play

[26]

besides gavottes and other trifling dances. Through his concertos, a form which he developed, he made a signal contribution to the art of writing for the orchestra. Indeed, Corelli is remembered as an outstanding pioneer, for he is credited with helping "to emancipate all instrumental music from the trammels of vocal style."

For almost thirty years Corelli lived at the palace of his patron, Cardinal Pietro Ottoboni. His weekly concerts there were the highlights of the cultural life of Rome, for the distinction of his music impressed his audiences deeply. It was for one of these concerts that Corelli composed his famous *Christmas Concerto*. The score of this work bears the inscription "Fatto per la Notte di Natale," but the listener will guess merely by listening to the polished ardor and tuneful yet majestic gravity of the work that this is real shepherd music, intended for performance on Christmas Eve.

FAHRENHEIT CONSTRUCTS THERMOMETER

OTHER EVENTS: Europe struggles over balance of power in War of Spanish Succession. Indians still undisturbed in Vermont. Queen Anne grants patent for first typewriter as England witnesses last execution for witchcraft. Brazil is world's chief supplier of gold. Liverpool is thriving center of West Indian slave trade. Reign of Louis XIV, Grand Monarch of France, draws to a close. Rococo, the age of the arabesque, begins. Couperin composes . . .

LEÇON DE TENEBRES NO. 3 (SEE PAGE 183).

During the 17th and 18th centuries many of Europe's monarchs maintained a Royal Chapel. This was much more than a royal place of worship. It was an institution employing, among others, many musicians—singers, organists, choristers, composers—so that the monarch might acquit himself of his religious duties to the accompaniment of the very best music.

When Thomelin, one of the four organists employed at the Royal Chapel of Louis XIV, died in 1678, the French monarch called in the applicants for the vacated job and listened to them play. He chose "as the most experienced in this exercise" a young man, Francois Couperin, descendant of a family of professional musicians. The young organist stayed with the King for years. In time he came to be nicknamed "Le Grand" to distinguish him from other members of his family.

Couperin composed several "Royal Concerts," some organ music, and many delicately etched harpsichord pieces by which he is primarily remembered. More revealing are his religious works—intricate with ornament but so direct and bold they will astound even the most sophisticated modern listener. Among these sacred compositions, one of the most poignant and unforgettable, is the *Leçon*, or *Service, of the Shadows No. 3*, so named because it was intended for performance during a liturgy that ended at nightfall.

TIBET, TRIBUTARY OF CHINA

OTHER EVENTS: Frenchman Bienville sets party of convicts to clear swamp for site of New Orleans. John Wesley founds Methodism at Oxford. Defoe's "Robinson Crusoe" runs through several editions. Tulip gardens the rage in Turkey; Sultan and Grand Vizier let duties slide for new hobby. All children ordered to attend school in Prussia. "Gulliver's Travels" published anonymously. Hot water heating introduced in French chicken hatchery. Bach composes . . .

CONCERTO IN D MINOR FOR TWO VIOLINS AND ORCHESTRA (SEE PAGE 175).

About the time when Johann Sebastian Bach was reaching maturity, secular instrumental music, still the backwash of the profession, was beginning to show signs of life. Couperin's new keyboard style was being widely studied; Corelli's concertos had just become available. This is one of the reasons why Bach, an organist at the Duke's chapel at Weimar in Central Germany, decided in 1717 to switch to the service of Prince

Leopold in nearby Göthen, even though Göthen
lacked a good organ. The Prince was an orchestral devotee, and the job he offered Bach
was that of Kapellmeister of his court orchestra
of 18 players. For Bach, who had so far composed chiefly for the organ, this was a not-to-be-
missed opportunity to experiment in the orchestral field.

Bach took the job and turned his five and a
half years at Göthen to good account. During
this period he produced his best orchestral
works, among them his *Brandenburg Concertos*
and his *Concerto For Two Violins*. In spite of
this, Bach in his day was not considered particularly outstanding, for he invented nothing
new. It is therefore hardly surprising that when
he died his music was forgotten and that a century elapsed before his art was rediscovered,
henceforth to be treasured as a complete sum-
mation of the musical ideas and resources of
his age.

FREEDOM OF PRESS IN NEW ENGLAND

OTHER EVENTS: English champion Jack Broughton invents boxing gloves. Italian Pergolesi creates first comic opera. Lord ("Turnip") Townsend revolutionizes agriculture with four-course system of rotating crops. British philanthropist, Oglethorpe, moves destitute across Atlantic to found Georgia. Benjamin Franklin's "Poor Richard's Almanack" is colonists' chief source of entertainment. Conscription introduced in Prussia. Handel composes . . .

ALCINA; BALLET-OPERA (SEE PAGE 189).

In George Frederick Händel we meet a personality which contrasts sharply with that of Johann Sebastian Bach. Both of these giants of 18th century music were born the same year, and both were reared in the same Protestant German lower middle class environment. But whereas Bach remained provincial and God-fearing and pennypinching, Händel developed into the elegant, much traveled caterer to aristocracy; and whereas Bach became the obscure but solid craftsman specializing in music of instrumental character, Händel won fame and fortune in the fields of opera and oratorio without troubling to learn the art of slow, painstaking workmanship—a flaw for which he is today paying the penalty of relative neglect.

His father was a barber in the service of a nobleman, and in deference to parental wishes, Händel studied the law. Soon, however, he switched to composition, for music poured out of him in a great stream, law or no law. At twenty-one he traveled to Italy where the performance of his music brought him fame and influential friends. Capitalizing on this success, Händel went to England. There he was feted, became naturalized, and produced many oratorios and operas. Among the latter *Alcina* is probably his best, for in this work Händel deftly combined the sensuousness of style which he had learned in Italy with a robust, envigorating gracefulness that is peculiarly his own.

CHIPPENDALE SETS FURNITURE STYLE

OTHER EVENTS: Frederick the Great, assiduous flutist, ascends Prussian throne; "he's hard to accompany," complain musicians of the court. With a kite Benjamin Franklin taps thundercloud; invents lightning rod. At garden party, British hear "Rule Britannia" a novelty by Arne. Casanova, of romantic fame, makes his 1st conquest. A Berlin scientist, Marggraf, introduces the microscope in chemical analysis; discovers sugar in beetroot. Rameau composes . . .

LES FÊTES D'HEBÉ (see page 198).

During the first half of the 18th century the orchestra undergoes two important changes in its make-up. The more versatile, horizontally held flute is substituted for the earlier "beaked" variety; and the French horn is introduced. Händel is among the first to realize and use the "noble sweetness" of the French horn, but the credit for writing the first truly melodious passages for the new instrument goes to Rameau.

By nature proud, reserved, and unapproachable, Jean Philippe Rameau emerges from obscurity as a young French organist who is determined to survey and re-appraise musical theory. At forty he is still unknown, but within the next few years he produces two pioneering treatises on harmony and some short pieces for the stage which cause a flurry of excitement. Conservative musicians attack him for his "strange chords;" they accuse him of being "a cold-blooded manufacturer of cacophonous music," and they are further scandalized when he composes an opera, then a ballet, then other operas. But now the public has rallied to his support, and the production of the ballet *Les Fêtes D'Hebé* sets the seal of his success as a composer.

This, briefly, is the story of Rameau, whose music we enjoy today because it is invariably fresh and full of spirit; and whose theoretical researches we recognize as the labor of an important pioneer.

PRIESTLEY DISCOVERS OXYGEN

OTHER EVENTS: Three big neighbors begin Poland's elimination from Europe's map. In Nottingham, Arkwright, inventor of the spinning frame, sets up first cotton mill. The cry of "riotous" is raised as a new dance, the waltz, is introduced. Australia is claimed for British Crown by Capt. Cook. With English in hot pursuit, music engraver Paul Revere gallops to Lexington. Parisians flock to first restaurant, in rue des Poulies. Gluck composes . . .

IPHIGENIE EN AULIDE; OPERA IN THREE ACTS (SEE PAGE 188).

When Marie Antoinette heard that Benjamin Franklin, American Ambassador at the court of Louis XVI, had declared himself in favor of the highly controversial Gluck, she is said to have remarked: "What does this man whose *métier* is to place rods on buildings know about music?"

At the time, feeling was running high at the French capital. *Iphigenie en Aulide,* embodying Gluck's essential operatic reforms had just been heard (1774) and had created a furore. The excitement was natural. For some time it had been felt that French opera was being sapped of its vitality by stale dramatic declamation; that Italian opera had been undermined as art through its extravagant displays of vocal virtuosity. Reform was clearly indicated, but when the reformer appeared, Paris split into two arguing camps—for and against Gluck. Yet what this noted German-Bohemian composer from Vienna was offering the public was the essence of reasonableness. He advocated a return to dramatic truth. The story of the opera, he said, must be simple; and as for the music, it must support the story, not interrupt it.

It is through the successful application of this ideal that Gluck became known as opera's Great Reformer, but it is through his eloquent music that he is remembered.

1769-75

WASHINGTON MAN OF THE HOUR

OTHER EVENTS: Watt's improvement of the steam engine heralds dawn of modern industrial era in England. Universal History, publ. in London, fixes date of Creation as Sept. 21, 4004 B.C. Gibbon's "Decline and Fall of Roman Empire" sees world as a struggle between barbarism and civilization. Massachusetts constitution declares that "all men are born free and equal." Torture still in use in King George III's Hanoverian possessions. Mozart composes . . .

SYMPHONY NO. 34 IN C MAJOR; —K-338

(SEE PAGE 196).

In Mozart's time the opera was a going institution and the operatic orchestra therefore commanded an impressive array of players. The so-called concert orchestra, on the other hand, was smaller and less elaborate. It was still a fledgeling, just barely emerging from its subservient status as a band hired by the wealthy nobleman, to become a public form of entertainment. Most of the new instruments, as they came along—the piccolo, the harp, the English horn, and others—therefore naturally found their way first into opera. It was only later and with some difficulty that they were admitted as ranking members of the concert orchestra.

The clarinet, for instance, though one of Mozart's loves, was used by him in only five of his forty-odd symphonies. It was not yet generally available; hence, Mozart deemed it prudent to dispense with it in many of his concert pieces—as witness his delightful (though clarinet-less) *Symphony in C Major* (K–338), characterized by critics as his first mature symphony.

Many have praised this lovely, delicately chiseled work. None has described it so aptly as Henri Ghéon who said that "Mozart never wrote anything that was firmer, more flowing, or more perfectly balanced, halfway between amusement and conviction, subtlety and ardor, grace and strength."

MARSEILLAISE TUNE OF THE HOUR

OTHER EVENTS: Two Frenchmen attract attention: Dr. Guillotin for advocacy of decapitating machine; Dr. Pinel for being first to strike shackles from the insane. In portraits of Spanish royalty Goya adds biting comment to gallery of contemporary life. France proclaimed a republic; Louis XVI and Marie Antoinette beheaded. News of mutiny on H. M. S. Bounty reaches Europe. A young general, Napoleon Bonaparte, comes to the fore. Haydn composes

SYMPHONY NO. 102 IN B-FLAT MAJOR;
SALOMON SERIES NO. 9 (SEE PAGE 190).

For almost thirty years Franz Joseph Haydn served as Kapellmeister in the household of the Prince of Esterhazy, composing and conducting music for the exclusive pleasure of his powerful employer. Held virtually a prisoner on the sumptuous estate of the Hungarian nobleman, he could not come and go at will; he could not mingle with the guests; when he conducted he had to wear a pigtail wig and a blue uniform with silver buttons. Yet he enjoyed certain advantages and opportunities which even today's composer might well envy.

Haydn had charge of a large musical establishment—a choir, solo singers, and an efficient little orchestra of some two dozen players. His opportunities for testing and experimenting were unequalled, and he enjoyed an audience of connoisseurs, for the Esterhazys were ardent music lovers.

When his employer died, Haydn emerged from his long years of isolation a complete master of his art. At the invitation of the impressario Salomon, he went to London and there produced his twelve greatest symphonies. These are magnificent considered as sheer music. But they are also notable for their dramatic scope, as if Haydn, dissatisfied with the perfumed environment of the palace, were searching valiantly for deeper truths than he had ever touched before.

MDCCC

THE NINETEENTH—

In this century, more than in any previous period, music is affected by the course of political events; is made to feel the impact of social change. For this is an age of stir and unrest and shifting values, of more "things" for more people; of strong currents of liberalism, of morality, of intense nationalism.

But above all it is the age of the middle class —the vast bourgeoisie of substantial families grown out of the Industrial Revolution; out of the flourishing colonial trade centering in the growing cities and towns.

The century opens with all of Europe's monarchs trembling before the revolutionary tide unleashed by France; setting their wills—the wills of absolute authority—against any symptom of this plague in their own countries. To protect Europe and the delicate balance of power that sustains each of them in his own

Divine Right—this is their task, and each goes at it with vigor.

First they have to deal with the meteoric Napoleon, who, having strengthened France with reforms, marches his conquering armies across Europe. He seems invincible—invading territories, extending French influence over vast areas, undertaking the conquest of Russia and failing, yet fighting on toward a new world, a Europe dominated by France.

After ten years they have stopped him. Absolute monarchy and the balance of power have won for the day. The revolutionary tide has been stemmed. Now the Holy Alliance between Russia, Austria, and Prussia is keeping revolt at bay by holding Europe together in peace; by suppressing any little rise of liberal tendency, and undoing whatever mild reforms may have crept in to undermine authority.

There are forty years of this enforced truce, and then a great eruption boils up beyond the power of the monarchs to suppress. The social, religious, and political ideas which have been fermenting, force their way to the surface. A new spirit of nationalism sweeps Europe. Out of it comes a formidable new world power, the German Empire, a union of German states under Prussia. In the South, the Spanish and Austrian dominated Italian states have risen to unite under Victor Emmanuel. In the East, the Serbs, the Magyars, and the Bulgars are battling their Turk and Austrian masters.

Turmoil enough for these power-balancing monarchs. But there is more. Underlying these nationalistic outbreaks, liberty is on the march again. France has overthrown the Orleans monarchy; it is once more a Republic. And as the social gales of 1848 subside, the middle class emerges as a dominant force; the real power behind the throne. Its growing influence has gone hand in hand with vital change and reform.

Parliamentary institutions have edged their way into almost every country. Religious tolerance is becoming a mark of civilization, and the ideals of personal liberty and freedom of thought have taken root. Slavery has been abolished, first in England and her possessions, then in all Europe, including Russia—then in America. Free elementary education, starting in Prussia, is spreading over the Western world.

Along with this has come a change of pace in the everyday life of the average man. Science, invention and the arts, but particularly invention, have made great strides. The introduction of steam and the railroad, the telephone and telegraph, agricultural machinery, industrial machinery, typewriters and sewing machines have one by one profoundly affected the habits and thoughts of the individual.

[44]

The middle class has had a hand in all of this. Its prosperous merchant families, having acquired wealth, have begun to look beyond mere trade. Hungry for culture and cultural prestige, they have reached out to painting, literature, and the other arts. Their influence on music is profound, for they bring to it a new audience and a new source of patronage. Instrumental music, almost completely eclipsed by opera and economically stranded through a gradual decline in aristocratic patronage, stands sadly in need of this support.

Early in the century, instrumental players are held in slight esteem, and composers cannot hope to make much of a living, let alone gain fame and fortune, except through opera. The few orchestras giving public concerts are not only inferior in the quality of their performance, but are expected to play "symphonies without tears," sandwiching popular songs between the movements.

These early 19th century orchestras are still patterned after the Classical model, comprising some fifty players—approximately half the number of performers used today. Beethoven sticks pretty closely to this standard cast. In the woodwind group he uses flutes, oboes, bassoons, and clarinets, in pairs. In the brass section he employs two French horns and two trumpets; in the percussion, a pair of kettledrums. But he increases the string section, and he assigns difficult solos to instruments, such as the double basses, previously heard only as parts of the ensemble. Above all, in his dramatic use of his materials—his sudden thrusts of sound and sharp contrasts in volume—he intensifies orchestral language to express suspense and drama and tumultuous conflict.

In all of this Beethoven goes beyond his age. Though he commands respectful admiration, he is not really understood.

Nevertheless the times are changing. A widening audience makes the concert hall a growing institution. Enthusiastic crowds applaud a Paganini, a Liszt, a Rubinstein. Symphony orchestras are being founded in all large cities. The piano, perfected now to where it is commercially available, is bringing music, the music of Chopin, Mendelssohn, and Schumann, into every home. But these are just the outward signs of an expanding music world. Music itself is changing.

Composers are in revolt against the formalism, the rigid rules and artificiality into which Classicism had degenerated. In this revolt they draw support from literature, which has already been powerfully affected by the liberating influences growing out of the French Revolution. The writers of Romantic prose and poetry—Hoffmann, Goethe, Byron, Victor Hugo—are animated by a new emotional intensity, and this is carried over into music. For now these sister arts have drawn very close. Composers dabble in writing while writers try their hand at music making. All are caught up in the new symbolism, the heightened emotional pitch, the picturesque sentimentalism that characterize the Romantic Movement. They turn for inspiration to medieval times, to the days of knight errantry, to the treasure house of legend and history. Out of this common impulse in the arts come, among others, Rossini's *William Tell,* von Weber's *Der Freischütz,* Mendelssohn's *A Midsummer Night's Dream,* and the *Fantastic Symphony* of Berlioz.

The Romantic spirit, at first confined mainly to France and Germany, soon crosses into other countries heretofore musically silent. In Russia, in Bohemia, in Norway, composers saturate themselves in their country's folklore and folksong, and soon there are flourishing nationalistic schools of composition, producing Glinka, Moussorgsky, Smetana, Dvorak, and Grieg.

The orchestra, meanwhile, to meet the varied, highly individualistic demands of these composers, has been changing rapidly.

The Romanticists—von Weber, Berlioz, Mendelssohn, and Schumann—have inherited Beethoven's dynamic orchestra. They use it, however, not for the expression of universal conflict, as did Beethoven, but for the painting of a more personal emotion which springs from their exuberant flights of fancy into the picturesque aspects of nature. The French horn, for instance, linked in Beethoven's time with the heroic, comes to suggest something much more specific—the virgin forest, the enchanted lake, the lofty castle. The English horn, previously absent, is added for its plaintive voice; the harp for its metallic glitter. Increasingly mutes are brought in to hush the strings.

Change also is affecting form. Beethoven, finding the minuet of Haydn much too tame, has replaced it in the symphony with the more vital scherzo. Berlioz has invented the descriptive symphony—a symphony which frankly tells a tale. Liszt has evolved the symphonic poem—a continuous, one-movement "symphony" based on a literary or pictorial idea.

Reaching the highest peaks in both Romanticism and Nationalism, Richard Wagner is as Olympian a figure as one of his own pagan gods. In his monumental music dramas, the orchestra reaches a tonal sumptuousness truly overpowering in its impact.

But the Romantic Movement is reaching a climax. Its voice is growing shrill; its orchestras too huge; its subjects too fantastic. A halt sooner or later must be called, a fresh departure found.

And now the painters discover something new. Thanks to the work of scientists in explaining color as a breaking up of light waves, painters try daubing pigments on canvas, letting the spectator's eye do the mixing. They achieve striking results, and the poets take up the idea, to do with words what the painters had done with color. The composers, with Debussy in the vanguard, soon follow suit. Calling themselves impressionists, as did the painters, they produce works that are ephemeral, elusive, shimmering, yet strangely vivid.

Now the century has run its course. It has been rich and varied in its developments, and as it closes there is an abundance of music for every taste. In Italy people whistle the airs of Verdi and Rossini. In Vienna they linger over beer or coffee to listen to the strains of Strauss waltzes. The frolicsome satires of Gilbert and Sullivan have captivated London. Everywhere —in Paris, Boston, Budapest, Madrid, New York—symphony orchestras are playing to capacity audiences. Indeed it seems that a new era, a day of music for the generality, is drawing close.

NAPOLEON BECOMES EMPEROR

OTHER EVENTS: Dr. Jenner honored in Europe for discovery of vaccination. With presidential hand, Thos. Jefferson inoculates family, friends at Monticello. Traveling by carriage through Austria, France, Schopenhauer notes population's squalor, unrest. First locomotive in action carries load in Wales mining district. Dalton formulates atomic theory. New Jersey acts, completing abolition of slavery in Northern states. Beethoven composes . . .

SYMPHONY NO. 3 IN E-FLAT MAJOR; —"EROICA"—(SEE PAGE 176).

The *Eroica* Symphony is notable in many ways. First there is the legend of its dedication. This tells us that the democratically-minded Beethoven, mistaking Bonaparte for a kindred spirit, a symbol of emancipation, dedicated the symphony to him. When the republican First Consul proclaimed himself Emperor, Beethoven in a fit of disillusioned rage, tore up the first page of the score and wrote on a fresh sheet:

"Simphonia Eroica," to which he later added
—"composed to celebrate the memory of a great
man."

This is an interesting sidelight, but the significance of the *Eroica* reaches deeper. Although
removed in time only nine years from the last
symphony of Haydn, it marks a complete break
with the politeness of the drawing room.
Echoes of this envigorating but studied gracefulness are still perceptible in Beethoven's First
(1800) and Second (1802) symphonies, but with
the *Eroica* he comes out squarely into the world
of passionate emotion. For the first time we hear
the frenzied accents of courage and defiance, are
hurtled into the very depths of black despair,
are lifted to emerge triumphantly into the light
of final liberation. And with this symphony the
orchestra reaches full maturity—a voice that
speaks with tenderness, compassion, anguish,
humor, embracing all the hopes and joys and
sorrows of mankind.

GAS BEGINS REPLACING CANDLES

OTHER EVENTS: British Parliament restricts workday to 12 hours; bans exploitation of children. 11-year old Liszt gives 1st concert in Vienna; is rewarded with public kiss from Beethoven. People read Grimm's "Fairy Tales"; discuss Monroe Doctrine; applaud exploit of paddlewheeler "Savannah," 1st ship to cross Atlantic with help of steam. Walter Scott completes "Ivanhoe." First permanent photograph produced in France. von Weber composes . . .

DER FREISCHUTZ;—"THE MARKSMAN"— OPERA IN 3 ACTS (SEE PAGE 210).

To express the spirit of revolt that enters music in the early 19th century, composers make a new and daring use of the resources of the orchestra. In this von Weber, the first self-conscious Romanticist in music, and Beethoven, lead the way.

They use all of the instruments together to produce not merely loud but soft effects; build volume not by making the whole orchestra play louder, but by starting with a few instruments and adding others one by one. They introduce the element of suddenness in their transitions from loud to soft; shift unexpectedly from fast to slow; use pauses to achieve suspense and drama.

To obtain different color combinations, von Weber has experimented with subdivided violins from which he has obtained effects of irresistible onrushing motion. He has discovered the value of the clarinet and of the other woodwinds in sustained harmonies, has learned to score the brasses so that they sound full and sonorous and brilliant. He has, in fact, so clearly indicated the general direction along which other composers must travel that *Der Freischutz*—a landmark in its own right as the first opera of truly German coloring and feeling —becomes the point of departure from which many of the orchestral inspirations of Berlioz, Liszt, and even Wagner will be derived.

FIRST RAILROAD
STOCKTON
TO DARLINGTON

OTHER EVENTS: Webster's efforts rewarded with publication of Dictionary. "They are a slow and fashionable poison," writes Dr. Hugh Smith, early crusader against corsets. World is enriched by birth of two insurgent spirits, Ibsen and Tolstoy. Friction matches appear; people, delighted, call them "lucifers." Br. House of Commons recognizes workers' right to collective bargaining. Steam navigation on the Rhine begins. Schubert composes . . .

SYMPHONY NO. 9 IN C MAJOR (SEE PAGE 202).

The year that Franz Schubert wrote this work —the last and greatest of his symphonies—his life had only a few months to run. The year was one of overwork, financial struggle, and frustrated hopes of a vacation to escape the stifling summer heat of Vienna. Unfortunately Schubert had neither the money necessary for the trip nor any prospect of an invitation by anyone he knew, and so he plowed ahead, depressed and undernourished, until attacks of giddiness and finally typhus came to his rescue.

On the tombstone marking the grave where he was placed within a few feet of Beethoven, the legend was inscribed: "Music has here entombed a rich treasure, but fairer hopes." Yet so little was anyone aware of the greatness of the man that the five hundred odd manuscripts found in his room were valued at two dollars by the authorities making an inventory of his few belongings. And so the world's most gifted melodist came by his death, unnoticed and unrewarded—aged 31.

He never heard his last symphony. The work was slated to be played while he was still alive, but it was found "too difficult" at the first rehearsal, and was shelved. It lay forgotten for ten years and did not come to light until Robert Schumann discovered it and gave it to the world. The "symphony of heavenly length," he called it.

1824-28

BRAILLE SYSTEM FOR THE BLIND

OTHER EVENTS: Law inflicting death penalty in all cases of forgery partially abrogated by British Parliament. "Lenient," reads sentence as urchin in Moscow is branded with hot iron and lashed for stealing church property. "Godey's Lady's Book" is launched; becomes supreme U. S. arbiter of fashions and etiquette for 30 years. French seize Algiers from Turks; poor Parisian tailor, Thimmonier, invents the sewing machine. Berlioz composes . . .

FANTASTIC SYMPHONY (SEE PAGE 177).

One of the leading figures in the Romantic Movement, Berlioz, was also one of the greatest innovators in the history of the orchestra. Though disinherited by his father for daring to write music instead of studying medicine; though twice disappointed in love; though constantly harassed by professional musicians, Berlioz nevertheless went right ahead composing; and not merely composing but investigating the possibilities of the orchestra.

He rearranged the placement of the players on the concert platform; insisted on rehearsing the orchestra by families of instruments before rehearsing all together. He did away completely with "harmonic drudges"—instruments used only to fill in harmony; installed the English horn and the bass clarinet; used instruments in all possible combinations. If the violins could be employed in subdivided groups to procure different tonal blends, he argued, so could the double basses; if the customary pair of kettle-drums could produce tones of distinct pitch, why not use four kettledrums and play full chords on them.

Berlioz' reforms were so far-reaching they filled a book which later became a standard text. However, only in his *Fantastic Symphony*, commemorating his frustrated love for the actress Henrietta Smithson, did he create a work that has maintained its position as a popular masterpiece.

MAGAZINE PUNCH APPEARS

OTHER EVENTS: Steam line Prussia to Saxony opens rail transportation in Germany. Baseball developed from "One Old Cat" by Col. Doubleday. S/S Britannia, 1st Cunarder, reduces Atlantic crossing to 14 days. Foster's parents bemoan Stephen's "strange talent for musick." In Scotland, inventor Macmillan is prosecuted for "furious driving on roads"—on 1st pedal bicycle. Emerson writes "Essays"; Carlyle introduces them in England. Schumann composes . . .

SYMPHONY NO. 1 IN B-FLAT MAJOR;—
"SPRING"—(SEE PAGE 202).

Robert Schumann, one of the leading spirits in the Romantic Movement, was almost as skillful a writer as he was a composer. Through the medium of a bi-weekly which he founded, Schumann engaged ceaselessly in journalistic polemics, proclaiming and expounding the aims of Romanticism, flaying the standpatters in music, and fighting to bring recognition to struggling young composers (Chopin, Brahms, and a great many others). Because of an injury to one of his fingers resulting from excessive zeal in practicing, Schumann just missed becoming a great pianist. Thus frustrated he turned to composition and in this field immortalized his name.

Oddly enough, he seems to have been the only one among composers of the period to have had difficulty in writing for the orchestra: (his scoring to this day is the despair of the conductor because of its frequently ill-balanced, monotonous, and turgid texture). Yet what he lacked as an orchestrator, Schumann more than made up by the freshness, exuberance, and sheer overabundant youthfulness of his ideas. One has but to listen to such a work as the *"Spring" Symphony*, composed in an upsurge of inspiration following Schumann's marriage, to realize the richness of his poetic fancy and the delight of his impetuous rhythms and soaring melodies.

FIRST ETHER OPERATION

OTHER EVENTS: Art-loving Dresden hears Wagner's "Flying Dutchman." Dickens, on visit to New York, is taken through the Tombs. "Discourage barbarous practice," asks Queen Victoria, and dueling in army is forbidden. Pioneers of Rochdale set up 1st successful cooperative. "What hath God wrought," 1st public message to travel over wire. Sarah Bernhardt born in Paris. Dumas completes "Count of Monte Cristo." Mendelssohn composes . . .

CONCERTO IN E MINOR, OP. 64 FOR
VIOLIN AND ORCHESTRA (SEE PAGE 194).

"I should have informed you long ago, esteemed Herr Mendelssohn, of the success with which I performed your Violin Concerto. It won extraordinary favor and was unanimously declared to be one of the finest works of its kind." So wrote Ferdinand David, soloist at the first performance on March 13, 1845 of the work which was to become a classic in the repertoire of the concert stage.

Felix Mendelssohn

This news, however welcome, could not have come as a complete surprise, for Mendelssohn's success as a composer had been immediate and overwhelming. The exquisite finish of his music—its suave precision of form, its melodies, sparkling and fragrant, and its transparent radiance of orchestration—had brought all Europe to his feet.

Mendelssohn's success was brief. Frail in health and agonizing inwardly from the wounds inflicted by a world indifferent to his hypersensitive nature, he broke at thirty-eight; and when he died, the tide turned against him. He was accused of being shallow, effeminate, and over-sentimental.

Of late the tide has turned again, for we have rediscovered Mendelssohn. Today we find that this Romanticist, hiding under the cloak of Classicism, has real distinction and that the delicate but penetrating glow of his poetic fancy can be intensely satisfying.

SPIRITUALISM BORN IN U.S.A.

OTHER EVENTS: "This is the place," says Brigham Young as advance guard of Mormons reaches Great Salt Lake. Uprisings sweep Europe; Marx and Engels issue Communist Manifesto urging proletarians to unite. France elects Napoleon III, nephew of famous Emperor, president of 2nd Republic. First shipment of wheat to Chicago by rail opens U. S. mid-West granary. England struggles with cholera; ignores Chopin's last concert. Glinka composes . . .

KAMARINSKAYA; ORCHESTRAL FANTASIA (SEE PAGE 187).

In Glinka's youth, Russia was still musically gagged, for it was ruled by the Italians. This domination began in the 17th century when Peri's *Dafne* was brought to Russia, implanting the belief that opera was a form of art in which Italian musicians only were qualified to deal (see pages 7, 12, and 22). For the century and a half that followed, all music in Russia bore the Italian label and nothing else was

[62]

tolerated, not even from native born composers.

Glinka, a well-to-do aristocrat who dabbled in music, was the first to depart from the familiar pattern. Like many others he started out by visiting Naples and Milan to steep himself in the Italian idiom. Unlike others he began to suffer from what he called "musical homesickness"—a wish to hear and to create a music that would express the temperament of his own countrymen.

Hastening back to Russia, Glinka set himself the task of recasting the primitive musical speech of the people—the Russian folksong—into a polished idiom acceptable as art. By this resolve and through the works that flowed from it—the sprightly *Kamarinskaya* and the two operas *Life for the Tsar* and *Russlan and Ludmilla*—Glinka became the father of his country's music and laid the foundation from which a truly national Russian music sprang and flowered.

FIRST STEINWAY PIANOS

OTHER EVENTS: H. Beecher Stowe's "Uncle Tom's Cabin" read by the million; translated into 23 languages. Tsar Alexander II begins emancipation of Russian serfs. Bessemer's invention gives world power to make steel cheaply. Crimean War, through Florence Nightingale, contributes beginning of nursing. "Fermentation due to tiny organisms," Pasteur tells skeptical world. The hoop skirt appears. Monte Carlo roulette begins to spin. Liszt composes

FAUST SYMPHONY (SEE PAGE 193).

Many composers have set to music Goethe's *Faust*, but none has done it as convincingly as Liszt. He alone seems to have captured the poem's mood, summed up its characters convincingly and deftly: Faust, preoccupied and questioning; Marguerita, serene and sweet; Mephistopheles, fiendish in his sarcasm. Indeed, to those who associate the name of Liszt with glistening display, the wealth of musical content and the emotional intensity of this work will come as a distinct surprise—a surprise made double by the composer's rich and brilliant orchestration.

Unlike Schumann, Liszt seems to have had no difficulty whatever in acquiring the habit of orchestral speech—as little difficulty as anything else he touched in music; and he touched many things. He was the first great virtuoso of the piano, and through his hands passed practically all the outstanding young pianists of the day, for Liszt was also a great teacher. Legendary, too, is the encouragement and· help which he gave freely yet wisely to promising composers; the volume and quality of the music which he himself composed.

For over half a century Liszt's influence was felt wherever music was composed or played, and though it later became fashionable to belittle his accomplishments history shows that he was one of the most dynamic and towering figures of the Romantic era.

1853-58

DARWIN'S THEORY OF EVOLUTION

OTHER EVENTS: East India Company ceases to rule as Britain annexes India. "House divided against itself cannot stand," says Lincoln. Barrel organs appear in streets of Europe. Pony Express makes initial run St. Joseph, Mo. to Pacific Coast. "Glory to God in the highest; on earth peace, good will toward men," reads 1st telegraphic message across Atlantic; cable fails after 17 days. Paris hears famous opera, Gounod's "Faust." Wagner composes . . .

TRISTAN AND ISOLDE; MUSIC DRAMA IN THREE ACTS (SEE PAGE 209).

(SEE PAGE 209).

Following in the footsteps of Gluck, Wagner made every element of opera, including his handling of the orchestra, subservient to the action on the stage. But since the whole conception of his music dramas was grandiose, he found the standard orchestra inadequate and set about inflating it.

Where previously three harps had been considered ample, he called for six; instead of the traditional four horns, he wanted eight. Eventually he wound up with a body of 112 players capable of thunderous sound effects. However, the use that Wagner made of this potential volume was as skillful as it was new. For instance, instead of swelling or decreasing volume with the whole orchestra, he wove a complicated pattern of alternating crescendos and diminuendos by individual instruments. He also introduced tiny melodic fragments intended not so much to be heard separately as to add greater richness to the tonal texture. In his climaxes he made the violins move in an intricate network of figuration around the blaring brasses which he did not hesitate to use in unison.

With *Tristan and Isolde*, Wagner reached full maturity. And the orchestra, responding to his master touch, now gave forth a sumptuousness of moving, blending, inter-weaving sounds the like of which had never been conceived, let alone heard, before.

ALICE IN WONDERLAND

OTHER EVENTS: Defying Paris academi-cians, Napoleon III tells insurgent painters: "Form rival 'Exhibit of the Refused.'" Viewing Monet's canvas "Impressions" journalist coins term "impressionism." Mrs. Eddy discovers Christian Science. Man with red flag must pre-cede mechanical vehicles on roads, says British law. Persian leader Baha Ullah lays groundwork of Bahai religion. Last shot fired in American Civil War. Balakireff composes . . .

THAMAR; SYMPHONIC POEM (SEE PAGE 176).

In Balakireff we meet with something new in music—a composer whose stature is measured not so much by his creative output as by his influence, through others, on the music of his time and country.

From Glinka, Balakireff caught the spark of Nationalism; the inspiration to create music truly Russian. This spark he passed on to a small group of gifted amateurs, among them Borodin, and Moussorgsky, and Rimsky-Korsakoff. He prodded these composers, praised or scolded them whenever necessary, gave them ideas and technical assistance, encouraged them and helped them to clarify their aims. His broader cultural and musical background, his keen intelligence, but particularly his magnetic ardor and unerring critical sense, made him their leader. Thus he became the spearhead of the Nationalist Movement through which he influenced the course of subsequent Russian music.

As a composer Balakireff is remembered by a few works, all of which show a gift of melody and the capacity to speak with fire. Particularly outstanding are his two semi-oriental tone poems, *Thamar* and *Islamei*. The former tells the story of the Caucasian vampire Queen Thamar who, after luring strangers to her castle, seduced them and had them killed and thrown into the foaming waters of the river Terek.

NOBEL
INTRODUCES
DYNAMITE

OTHER EVENTS: Joseph Lister's use of ster-ilization spray sharply reduces mortality during operations. At instigation of fishing interests U. S. buys "Russian America" (Alaska); public more interested in newly laid Transatlantic cable, establishing lasting contact with Europe by wire. Karl Marx writes "Das Kapital" stat-ing doctrine of class struggle. Emperor Maxi-milian of Mexico courtmartialed and shot by Republican forces. Moussorgsky composes . . .

BORIS GODOUNOV; MUSICAL FOLK DRAMA
IN THREE ACTS (SEE PAGE 195).

In 1868 Modeste Moussorgsky obtained a job as a government clerk—only to find his days slipping away in fretful phrasing and rephrasing of inconsequential official documents. This was the year when he began the composition of his great national epic dealing with the ill-fortunes of the scheming usurper, Tsar Boris. On this labor he staked his hopes and lavished his best thoughts and every minute of his spare time.

When *Boris* was finally completed, Moussorgsky submitted it to the directors of the Imperial Opera. But the directors failed to appreciate the intensity of the new work, its plangent melodies, its fateful brooding silences. Unanimously they rejected it. It lacked, they said, a leading female part. It was eccentric, unplayable. The subdivision of the double basses, they complained, was contrary to all known rules of orchestration.

Nevertheless, in 1874 *Boris Godounov* was finally produced—for a few nights—and then withdrawn in spite of popular approval, and soon forgotten. Later, Rimsky-Korsakoff revised it, touching it up to make it "playable"; and in this form it reappeared in 1908 and was a great success. Not until 1928, however, was the original version of this now famous opera by Russia's most original composer exhumed and reinstated, thanks mainly to the efforts of the Soviet Government.

GERMAN EMPIRE PROCLAIMED

OTHER EVENTS: 68 vessels of all nations sail in festive array through 100 miles of newly opened Suez Canal. John D. Rockefeller and brother William found Standard Oil Co. People turn longing eyes to So. Africa as diamonds discovered at Kimberley. Paris surrender climaxes Franco-Prussian War. Chicago swept by disastrous fire. Lenin born 576 miles S. E. of Moscow. Last spike driven home in Union Pacific Railroad. Borodin begins composition of . . .

PRINCE IGOR; OPERA IN A PROLOGUE AND 4 ACTS (SEE PAGE 179).

Borodin's musical gifts were very different from those of either Moussorgsky or Rimsky-Korsakoff, his great colleagues among the Russian nationalists.

Borodin did not have Rimsky's command of theory or Moussorgsky's uncanny faculty of conjuring so much with a few deft strokes. But he had something else. His semi-Asiatic ancestry (he was Georgian by birth) enabled him to give expression to the sensuous, barbaric glamor of the East with perfect naturalness and conviction. His scientific turn of mind helped him to accommodate himself with greater ease than his colleagues to the principles underlying the structure of Western music. Thus he produced a unique blend—a music thoroughly Western in outward form yet truly Eastern in spirit.

It is a matter of real regret that such a gift should have been practiced as an avocation amidst the infinite distractions of a professional career. For Borodin was primarily a man of science. He lectured at the St. Petersburg Medical College, attended faculty meetings, wrote books on chemistry, and only at odd moments labored on his *Prince Igor*. This epic work recounting a legendary episode from Russia's period of subjection to the will of Tartar Khans, was left unfinished when Borodin died. It was completed by Rimsky-Korsakoff and Glazounoff.

TYPEWRITER BECOMES PRACTICAL

OTHER EVENTS: Ex-Emperor Napoleon III dies an exile in England; France more interested in adventures of Phileas Fog described in Jules Verne's sensationally successful book "Round the World in 80 Days." Republican Elephant, Democratic Donkey, Tammany Tiger created by cartoonist Nast in Harper's Weekly. Egypt gains virtual autonomy from Turkish Sultan. Two attempts made to reach Europe from America by balloon; both fail. Saint-Saëns composes . . .

CONCERTO (CELLO AND ORCHESTRA)
IN A MINOR OP. 33 (SEE PAGE 200).

During the 19th century, the adoption of new instruments as regular members of the symphony orchestra and the increase in the number of players, now close to one hundred odd, gradually tapered off and finally stopped. And at about the same time there emerged in the manner in which composers used the orchestra, distinct characteristics expressing not merely individual but national differences. The Germans, for instance, revealed a tendency toward heavy-handedness, especially in the middle voices, as in the case of Schumann; the Russians, from Glinka on, a love for bold, sharply contrasted color; the French, a certain lightness and fastidious elegance of touch as evidenced, for instance, in the familiar *Danse Macabre* by the eclectic, talented Saint-Saëns.

Saint-Saëns was a brilliant organist, an author and an educator as well as a prolific, versatile composer. But the very facility with which he wrote music, seeking lucidity rather than emotional content, prevented him from realizing to the full his extraordinary gifts. Occasionally, as in his opera, *Samson and Delilah*, in the *A Minor Cello Concerto* (a grand war horse in spite of its sentimentality) and in several other compositions, he achieved music of lasting merit. But for all these splendid works his influence on his contemporaries was very slight.

PARIS THÉÂTRE DE L'OPÉRA OPENS

OTHER EVENTS: Schliemann digs up first known relics of prehistoric Greece; exploit heralds dawn of modern archeology. "Spiritualist phenomena can be produced without aid of spooks," says Mme. Blavatsky, Russian world traveler, making demonstration; founds Theosophical Society. Bell succeeds in transmitting by wire the sound of a twanging clockspring; ushers in telephone invention. Englishman, Wingfield, devises lawn tennis. Bizet composes . . .

CARMEN; OPERA IN 4 ACTS (SEE PAGE 178).

Occasionally a work intended for the stage contains music of such originality or daring or vitality that it transcends the medium for which it was composed. By way of the symphony and the salon orchestra; today also by way of radio and phonograph, it reaches out to thrill an infinitely larger audience. *Carmen* is music of this type.

The personality of the alluring cigarette girl,

Carmen, caught Bizet's fancy, bringing out the best there was in him. Though in poor health, exhausted, and strained financially, he gave to the execution of the work infinite care. He re-wrote the brazen, supple *Habanera* 13 times, made dozens of small changes at rehearsals; and finally the opera was ready to come before the public. It was produced not at the magnificent new Paris Opéra, but at the smaller Opéra-Comique, for there was some trepidation lest its realism might arouse prudish opposition from a public accustomed to a more sentimental fare. These fears were justified. Although it ran for 37 nights, *Carmen's* success was at first indifferent. And as the curtain fell on the 23rd performance, Bizet died disconsolate, not knowing that he had produced a masterpiece.

It is of interest to note that Spaniards, though recognizing *Carmen's* many virtues, do not esteem it highly. Its "Spanishness" is not authentic, they believe.

EDISON INVENTS PHONOGRAPH

OTHER EVENTS: First railway opens in China; first great railroad strike ties up U. S. A. Queen Victoria proclaimed Empress of India; receives dress woven of spider web from Empress of Brazil. Johns Hopkins founded as U. S. takes up science. First telephones installed in London. Five women, alleged witches, burned alive at San Jacobo, Mexico. Custer makes last stand. "Anna Karenina" Tolstoy's 2nd great novel brings acclaim. Brahms composes . . .

SYMPHONY NO. 2 IN D MAJOR (SEE PAGE 179).

The bite and meatiness of the orchestral music of Johannes Brahms, its gruff yet mellow charm, and the inevitable feeling that it gives of being the expression of a great and honest soul, commanding our attention and our admiration, triumphed over its alleged weaknesses of scoring, austerity, and lack of popular appeal. Moving up steadily in the past fifty years, the four Brahms symphonies—classical in form, romantic in spirit, and cast in the grand manner—today stand at the very top in popular esteem.

Although the heroic *First Symphony* of Brahms was later to become the great popular favorite, it was with his gentler *Second Symphony* that the German master scored his first real triumph. This symphony, conceived during a stay at Pörtschach on the lake of Wörth fairly radiates the friendliness of the Austrian countryside.

When Billroth, a friend of Brahms, heard the symphony, he exclaimed: "It is all rippling streams, blue sky, sunshine, and cool green shadows. How beautiful it must be at Pörtschach!" And beautiful it must have been, for Brahms returned there again and again to watch "how all the mountains round the blue lake are white with snow, while the trees are covered with delicate green."

The work, idyllic and delicately contemplative, is Brahms' "Pastoral" symphony.

GILBERT & SULLIVAN'S H.M.S. PINAFORE

OTHER EVENTS: First truly automatic machine gun demonstrated by inventor Maxim; "Too expensive in ammunition," says wistful Chinese envoy. Whistler scores legal victory for impressionism in painting; collects damages from Ruskin for criticism of work. Bismarck cracks down on liberal Germans. Loose contact in telephone receiver leads D. Hughes to invention of microphone. Booth's revivalist mission becomes Salvation Army. Dvořák composes . . .

SLAVONIC DANCES (SEE PAGE 184).

Like many another oppressed country, Bohemia (now Czecho-Slovakia) felt the strong undertow of national political feeling that swept all Europe in the middle 19th century. And it responded by producing two outstanding composers—Smetana and Dvořák—both of whom, through their music, prepared the people for their day of independence.

Dvořák, the younger of the two, was the son of a butcher, but he early learned to play the

viola and organ. As a struggling young composer he wrote two sets of *Slavonic Dances* whose
vigor and folkish charm made him famous—
and popular enough to become suspect by the
authorities. The Czechs, in later years, won
their independence, then lost it; and today
Dvorák is again considered dangerous and subversive. Commenting on this fact, the New
York Times said editorially on September 9th,
1941:

"The hundredth anniversary of the birth of
Antonin Dvorák was remembered in Czecho-
Slovakia yesterday, but the Nazi trespassers and
their Quislings did not allow it to be publicly
celebrated. . . ." Dvorák "loved too much the
folk songs, dances and lore of his native land,
put into his music too much of the free and
proud Bohemian spirit. He glorified the joys
and sorrows of humble people, and this, under
present conditions in Bohemia, can hardly be
allowed."

1878

WOOLWORTH OPENS 5 & 10c STORE

OTHER EVENTS: Edison constructs electric bulb, fascinated, unable to sleep, watches invention as lamp burns 45 hours. King of Bavaria, in water chariot, has himself drawn about mountain lake by trained swans to strains of Wagner; "strange" says British Register. Ibsen writes "Doll's House"; is assailed for questioning sanctity of loveless marriage. Czechs abandon passive resistance; elect 36 deputies in Austrian election. Smetana composes . . .

MA VLAST;—"MY COUNTRY"—CYCLE OF SIX SYMPHONIC POEMS (SEE PAGE 205).

From early manhood Smetana resented the German schooling to which, as a native of Bohemia, he had been subjected in childhood; and this resentment made him take an active part in the revolution of 1848 to free his country from the rule of Austria.

The revolution came to nothing, but the patriotic fire that had flared up in Smetana continued to burn fiercely. He became a composer

—and a national hero. For in his music the Czech peasant and shopkeeper, the soldier and the noble all recognized a familiar native strain that quickened their pulse and made them conscious of their common heritage of temperament and aspiration.

When Smetana composed his opera, *The Bartered Bride,* the melodies from this lively work were picked up and whistled in every hamlet of the land; and each subsequent work was greeted by the people as though it were indeed not merely music but a symbol of emancipation. The greatest of these works, *Ma Vlast,* is a symphonic cycle which celebrates in tone the beauty of Bohemia and its legendary past. Because of its broad sweep of melody and stirring sincerity of feeling, this work marks one of the highest poetic peaks of 19th century music. Is was composed a few years before Smetana's death, when illness and overwork had already sapped his strength and rendered him stone deaf.

BUSTLE APPEARS IN FEMININE FASHIONS

OTHER EVENTS: Repressive Capt. Boycott is hemmed in on estate by Irish villagers; incident enriches language with new term. Spain takes steps to abolish slavery in Cuba as unrest fails to subside. "In perfect condition," declares Queen Victoria sampling 1st shipment of frozen meat from Australia. Russian magazine prints first installment of new serial "Brothers Karamazov." Niagara Falls harnessed; electric power illuminates park. Tchaikowsky composes . . .

SERENADE IN C MAJOR FOR STRING ORCHESTRA, OP. 48 (SEE PAGE 207).

In the bassoon and the bass clarinet, Tchaikowsky found a capacity for the expression of sepulchral anguish and foreboding that fitted in exactly with his misanthropic, brooding nature. He naturally made a new and telling use of these two instruments, producing with their help a poignancy of mood new to music.

Add to this that he was an arch Romanticist living at the high tide of the Romantic era; a

[84]

Russian with a typically Russian and, in music. a decidedly novel disposition to alternate abruptly between intense despair and buoyant joy—that he was in addition a melodist of the first water and an unusually brilliant orchestrator, and the reasons are apparent for his being the first Russian composer to become known throughout the world.

Somewhere between the composition of his *Fourth* and *Fifth Symphonies*, Tchaikowsky was commissioned to write the showy *1812 Overture*. As if to atone for this concession to vulgar taste, he undertook at the same time the composition of his *Serenade for Strings*. In a letter he indicated plainly what he thought of these two compositions:

"The Overture," he wrote, "is of local interest and noisy. I wrote it without warmth or enthusiasm. The Serenade, on the contrary, came from an inner impulse, and I put into it the best there was in me."

FRENCH
DIG
PANAMA CANAL

OTHER EVENTS: Tsar Alexander II abolishes poll tax; is shot in street on day he signs liberal proposal leading to constitution. Paris applauds premiere of Offenbach's "Tales of Hoffmann." "Please refrain from shooting game from car windows," Union-Pacific posts on its billboards. A. F. of L. founded at Pittsburgh labor convention. Vatican archives opened to historians. Pres. Garfield assassinated by disappointed office seeker. Grieg composes . . .

FOUR NORWEGIAN DANCES, OP. 35 (SEE PAGE 189).

So strong ran the tide of Nationalism in the 19th century that even the Norwegians, a people not given to mixing in Europe's turmoil, caught the fever. In the nationalist writers Bjornson and Ibsen, and in the nationalist composer Edvard Grieg, they produced outstanding figures who gave eloquent testimony to the rugged heartiness and resolute independence of their race.

Grieg's first compositions gave no inkling of all this. But early his path crossed with that of Norway's first nationalist composer, Richard Nordraak, whose vision of a "national Norse music" inspired by the Norwegian folksong, fired Grieg's imagination. Soon young Nordraak died, his genius unfulfilled, but Grieg carried on, composing music of such heroic glow that he endeared himself to people the world over.

Grieg loved his native countryside. He seemed happiest when able to retreat to a small cabin perched on a mountain slope near the Hardanger Fjord. For in his music it is this sturdy country he expressed—rural, remote, and cold but inhabited by men and women of bold, venturesome spirit. This close communion with the native soil permeates all of Grieg's music. Nowhere is it more strongly felt than in his *Four Norwegian Dances, Op. 35*, surely one of the most vivid compositions he ever wrote.

R. L. STEVENSON'S
TREASURE
ISLAND

OTHER EVENTS: German scientist Koch isolates tuberculosis germ. U. S. places ban on Chinese immigration; incommodes Mormons with anti-polygamy bill. France withdraws from dual rule of Egypt; leaves Britain in full control. Millionaire patrons outshine singers as Metropolitan Opera House opens. Houdini, "Handcuff King" begins career as trapeze artist. Brooklyn Bridge completed. Horse and buggy era about to wane. Franklin D. Roosevelt born. Chabrier composes . . .

ESPAÑA; A RHAPSODY (SEE PAGE 181).

In Chabrier, the composer, we sense the same exuberant if somewhat vulgar boisterousness that characterized every word and gesture of Chabrier the man—a fabulous character if we are to believe the legend that still trails his memory.

An offspring of provincial, bourgeois France, Chabrier came to Paris as a youngster. He studied the law, became a government function-

ary, then turned to music and eventually re-
signed his Civil Service post. Now 39, ambitious
but largely self-taught, he launched himself into
composition with all the bursting and tumultuous energy which had already brought him
notoriety. For he was now a well known figure
at the capital. "His theatrical gestures," says
James Hadley, "his homeric bursts of laughter,
the unbelievable items of his apparel—gorgeous
waistcoats, outlandish hats; the fantastic tales
with which he regaled his friends and neighbors
—all of these had made him the undisputed
king of the Bohemian life of Paris."

When Chabrier produced his rhapsody *España* he scored a triumph, for in this work he
had combined a zest, a glow, and an ebullient,
robust humor quite irresistible. Today, seeing
beyond his antics as a man, we realize that
Chabrier was not merely a talented eccentric
but a composer of independence and integrity
and great originality.

FIRST ELECTRIC TROLLEYS

OTHER EVENTS: An American, William James, and a Dane, C. G. Lange, working independently, arrive at similar explanation of emotion. The French trade unions are recognized by legislature. An Englishman, J. W. Swan, and a Frenchman, H. de Chardonnet, working independently, discover artificial silk (rayon). In Germany, a gasoline-powered bicycle appears. Canadian-Pacific reaches coast-to-coast. Cremation legalized in England. César Franck composes . . .

SYMPHONIC VARIATIONS FOR PIANO AND ORCHESTRA (SEE PAGE 186).

Though born in Belgium, César Franck spent fifty-five years of his life in Paris and is therefore considered as being not a Belgian but a French composer. These years in Paris were hard, frugal, uneventful. Alternately attending to his duties as a church organist and crisscrossing Paris on foot to supplement his meager income by a few private lessons, Franck kept up an even tempo of existence—rising early, working straight through until bedtime—sustained and comforted by an intense desire to compose.

Slowly, over the years, snatching a few minutes here and a few minutes there, he wrote music. No one heard of him for a long time except as an organist famed for his improvisations. Few paid any attention to his music after they had become aware of its existence except to hold it up for ridicule. Uncomplaining, Franck went right on until he was knocked over by a bus at sixty-eight and died from pleurisy shortly thereafter.

In the decades that followed, the lofty nobility and strangely gripping mystic exaltation of Franck's music received belated recognition. His *Symphony* today tops the list of concert favorites, and his other mature works—the *Symphonic Variations* and a handful of other compositions—are recognized as the products of genius.

STATUE OF
LIBERTY
UNVEILED

OTHER EVENTS: Queen Victoria celebrates golden jubilee; performance of Wagner's "Lohengrin" in London canceled because of anti-German outcry. Nietzsche, in "Beyond Good and Evil" lacerates man's decadence. Charles Hall's experiments put aluminum on the market. Appearance of first Sears, Roebuck catalog begins mass distribution of city merchandise in U. S. ruralia. Earthquake wrecks Charleston; eyewitnesses describe ordeal. Fauré composes . . .

REQUIEM, OP. 48 (SEE PAGE 185).

Comparing Gabriel Fauré to other French composers, Roger Ducasse has called him "more profound and mysterious than Saint-Saëns, more spontaneous than d'Indy, more classical than Debussy." This glowing tribute is well deserved. Fauré's music is restrained and polished. It has the clarity of a deep mountain lake; the serenity of spiritual security; the tenderness that comes from mellowed human understanding.

Since these are qualities that are less easily

appreciated than display or outbursts of emotion, Fauré has suffered through the very virtues that made him great. Though one of the most influential figures in French music, he has remained one of the loneliest, and, outside of his own country, one of the most neglected of composers.

Throughout his life Fauré held, one after another, various posts as church organist in and around Paris; and, being a shy and modest man, he went quietly about his business. Gradually, however, he attracted notice as a composer, especially by the beauty of his songs and the originality and exquisite artistry of his chamber music.

In 1886 Fauré's father died. Deeply moved, the composer wrote a *Requiem* to express, as he put it, "my sincere and moving grief." This composition, lofty in mood and poignantly beautiful, is ranked as one of the finest religious works produced in France.

BRAZIL
ABOLISHES
SLAVERY

OTHER EVENTS: Explorer Nansen and five companions make first crossing of Greenland's inland ice. "Thanks," says Oxford Dictionary to 13,000 compilers on completion of 1st volume (begun in 1857). Pasteur Institute founded in Paris. Bellamy's vision of Utopia "Looking Backward, 2000–1887" a best-seller. French build 1st naval submarine. Great Blizzard buries Broadway in 6 ft. of snow. Relics of Mahomet found in Cairo. Rimsky-Korsakoff composes . . .

SCHEHERAZADE; SYMPHONIC SUITE AFTER
"THE 1001 NIGHTS" (SEE PAGE 199).

Orchestral players enjoy performing the music of Rimsky-Korsakoff; they give it their best effort. For the eminent Russian knew not only how to take advantage of the characteristics and capacities of the instruments for which he wrote; he never missed a chance to give the individual players something worth while and interesting to do.

Rimsky was trained to be a naval officer but he

soon joined the ranks of Balakireff, Moussorgsky, Borodin, and other ardent nationalists, and became a composer. To remedy the many glaring gaps in his equipment, discovered when he started teaching composition at the St. Petersburg Conservatory, Rimsky set himself the task of mastering musical theory. In time he became one of the most erudite minds in the profession.

Of the fifteen operas which Rimsky-Korsakoff composed, none, with the possible exception of *The Golden Cockerel,* has fared well outside of Russia. By contrast, his orchestral works have enjoyed great popularity. For although Rimsky did not overflow with natural, "spontaneous lyricism," he was a master orchestrator and knew how to display his wares to excellent advantage. When at his best he could work marvels—as in *Scheherazade,* as gorgeous an example of descriptive semi-oriental music as has come out of the whole Russian Nationalist Movement.

AUTOMOBILE BECOMES PRACTICAL

OTHER EVENTS: Eiffel Tower completed in time for Paris Exposition. Girl arrested in Central Park, New York, for riding a horse astride. Five thousand perish in Johnstown flood; assistance to victims ($3,742,818) sent from Europe, Asia, and Africa. In Austrian village, Alois Hitler congratulated by neighbors on birth of his son, Adolf. Montana, Washington, Dakotas, admitted to Statehood. Brazil proclaimed a republic. Richard Strauss composes . . .

DEATH AND TRANSFIGURATION; SYMPHONIC POEM (SEE PAGE 206).

When an orchestral player in Beethoven's time objected to a passage, protesting that it was unplayable, Beethoven is said to have exclaimed: "What do I care about your miserable violin!" For with Beethoven the idea came first, its execution second.

But as the orchestra developed into an instrument capable of infinite gradations of tonal color, a basic change of attitude emerged. Composers began thinking in terms of what the orchestra *might* do, and therefore showed a tendency to build their music less from an idea, rhythmic or melodic, than from a particular effect (such as trumpets playing staccato chords). Legend has it, for instance, that Richard Strauss used to sneak up on the players during intermission to hear them practicing when they thought they were unobserved; that in this manner he brought into his scores many things previously thought impossible.

Whether or not this story tallies with the facts, the wizardry of Strauss' scoring is undisputable. Couple this with the "cyclonic energy" of his music, as Debussy characterized it, and it is clear why in the century's closing years Strauss became supreme. During this period he produced his most outstanding works, among them the symphonic poem *Death and Transfiguration,* expressing the emotions experienced during an illness that came close to being fatal.

GIBSON
GIRL
ERA

OTHER EVENTS: Nicholas II, last Russian Tsar, ascends throne. "A bad omen," wiseacres say when thousands crushed as scaffolding under celebrants collapses. In England, elementary education is made compulsory and free. Ramsay discovers helium. Boos and hisses greet impressionism in music as Paris hears Debussy's "Afternoon of a Faun." To promote revolution Lenin gives up law practice. Strand Magazine presents Sherlock Holmes. Bruckner composes . . .

SYMPHONY NO. 9 IN D MINOR <small>(SEE PAGE</small>
180).

Although historians refer to the Austrian master, Anton Bruckner, as "the last giant of Romanticism," his works have suffered general neglect. They have aroused prolonged and heated controversy, but they are seldom played outside of Germany and Austria. The reason that music of such sturdy and forthright eloquence has failed to "take" may be that we have moved into an age in which discursiveness no longer fits. Or, possibly, we may not be acquainted with the composer's full intentions. For Bruckner suffered not only at the hands of critics and detractors who called him "half Caesar, half school teacher;" he was the victim of the excessive zeal of his admirers. The story of his Ninth Symphony illustrates the point.

When Bruckner died, this symphony, left unfinished, fell into the hands of Ferdinand Löwe. This ardent disciple, in his anxiety to have the work succeed, decided to edit it so as to smooth out the "rough spots." He filled in certain pauses, sandpapered the titanic dissonances of the scherzo, retouched even the haunting splendor of the adagio, thus severely damaging the composer's musical ideas. Since he performed this task anonymously and secretly, the revision was mistaken for the original, and thirty years passed before the mistake was rectified and Bruckner was allowed to speak for himself.

FREUD INTRODUCES PSYCHOANALYSIS

OTHER EVENTS: France annexes Madagascar. U. S. Rural Free Delivery brings world to the farmer's door. Browning invents automatic revolver. Automobiles in England may travel 12 m.p.h. Man will not soon get used to "speeding behind nothing," reflects N. Y. Times. German physicist Röentgen discovers the X-ray. Crane's "Red Badge of Courage" U. S. fiction landmark. Lumiere Brothers invent the cinema. Olympic games revived at Athens. Chausson composes . . .

POÈME FOR VIOLIN AND ORCHESTRA, OP. 25
(SEE PAGE 181).

Ernest Chausson was a happy yet frustrated man. His happiness lay in his beautiful young wife, his charming children, his home—a treasure house of rare books, pictures, and *objets d'art* which he had collected; it lay in his appreciation of the finer things of life, the generosities which wealth made possible. Yet somehow this visionary, this Frenchman of sensitive and passionate humanitarianism, was burdened by his own well-being, for it reminded him continuously that he was out of touch with life as it is lived in sweat and pain. He was almost ashamed of his fortunate position and dimly questioned his right to what he cherished most. This doubt made him do strange, unexpected things.

Instead of peddling his own works, he went to publishers and impressarios carrying under his arm the manuscripts of struggling composers; instead of talking about his own music, he laid before them the work of others. Yet his own compositions show him to have been unusually gifted. His songs, his *Symphony in B Flat Major*, his *Poem for Violin and Orchestra* (on which his reputation mainly rests) may be too delicate to attract a wide public. But they are firmly spun for all their gentleness; and their nostalgic glow and tenderly expressed emotion reveal great beauty and distinction.

1895-96

GOLD RUSH
TO THE YUKON

OTHER EVENTS: European Powers scramble for remaining bits in partition of Africa. U. S. battleship Maine blown up in Havana harbor. In India, Ronald Ross discovers that malaria is transmitted by mosquitoes. In Gladstone's death England loses a public man of "unique genius, character, and achievement." First Russian census uses clergy as enumerators. Diesel engine put into use. U. S. annexes Hawaii. Curies discover radium. MacDowell composes . . .

"INDIAN" SUITE; OP. 48 (SEE PAGE 194).

Edward MacDowell enjoys the distinction of being the first American composer to have made himself heard internationally.

He was a high-strung, energetic man with an inquiring and restless mind. Trained abroad but American by birth, tradition and impulse, MacDowell always wanted to know more about his country's past, its legends and its days of pioneering. This led him to undertake many long hikes through Maine, New Hampshire, and

Vermont. He tramped around the countryside with farmers, asked them a million questions, reconstructed the life of the early settlers, studied native lore and native music—and this is how he came eventually to write his well known *"Indian" Suite.*

In this work MacDowell sought to sum up the rude environment and the fiercely independent spirit of the North American Indian. Being a Romanticist, peculiarly fitted by temperament for dealing through music with the glamorous outdoors, he recreated the mood of mighty forest and rolling plain through which once strode the proud but savage Kiowas and Iroquois; and in the music he expressed as well the tenderness, the mysticism, and the romance that made the Red Man so unique. Though he composed a number of other outstanding works, MacDowell, shortly before he died, expressed a greater preference for this Suite than for any other of his compositions.

CANNED PINEAPPLE, A NOVELTY

OTHER EVENTS: Russian Govt. sponsors peace conference at the Hague; suppresses liberties in Finland. "Only Anglo-Saxons can govern themselves," writes Wm. Allen White adding voice to U. S. "manifest destiny" clamor. "Only when properly chaperoned," may girls venture forth after dark, etiquette books agree. Veblen's "Theory of a Leisure Class" dismissed. England launches conquest of Boer Republics; action denounced throughout civilized world. Elgar composes . . .

"ENIGMA" VARIATIONS (SEE PAGE 185).

The period of greatest glory in any art usually comes when its methods and possibilities have been fully grasped but its limitations not yet fully realized. This interesting observation made by Barrett Wendell, suggests a corollary: that the time and place of an artist's birth are often as important, even crucial, to the development of his creative faculties as are his natural endowment and technical equipment.

Sir Edward Elgar

Fate decreed that Elgar, an Englishman by birth and a Romanticist by disposition, should have appeared at a time when Romanticism had practically spent itself, and reached maturity in a country still conspicuous by its lack of interest in music. Elgar's struggle for recognition was therefore doubly hard; and even though he eventually won through and was showered with honors, his inner battle went on. He never did succeed in ridding his musical utterances completely from swagger and other self-conscious mannerisms that come from a feeling of being "out of step."

The turning point in Elgar's career came when he composed, at 42, the wonderfully rich and varied *"Enigma" Variations* which at one stroke reinstated the prestige of English orchestral music. The nickname "Enigma" derives from the fact that each variation is a musical portrait of one of Elgar's friends whose identity was not divulged.

THE TWENTIETH —

The first fourteen years of our own century seem to be on the other side of a sharp dividing line. In music no less than in world affairs the Great War of 1914 marks the end of a period; the beginning of a new impulse, a major shift, a radically different course.

In the first brief period music still draws its sustenance and inspiration from the past. It is dominated by the impressionism of Debussy, by the Romantic realism of Richard Strauss, by Nationalism which finds a late flowering in Vaughan Williams in England and Falla in Spain. Thereafter a new mood comes into music and gradually crystallizes into a new language—a language that strikes a sterner tone. Composers speak with greater terseness, avoid emotion, experiment with different forms. They throw out the established laws that have governed music up to now and they build from new bases, new harmonic conceptions. This revolution in music is a direct reflection of the world revolution in the affairs of man. It is a counterpart of the revulsion which is everywhere felt against the excesses of the past; and the changes which are swept in by this revulsion in world affairs and music coincide in time.

In the first years of the century there is little indication of all this. The age of power and speed and mass production is just dawning. The radio, the movie, the automobile, are all "in the works" but they are not yet here. Theodore Roosevelt is just now arranging for the Panama Canal. England is preoccupied with social reforms. International copyright laws and health agreements and postal service have everywhere been established. All Europe, having successfully used diplomacy and the conference table in the partition of Africa, now looks confidently toward an enlightened age of peace by arbitration. The world seems very bright to those who cannot see beneath the rosy surface.

Soon, however, rumors spread that there is trouble in the "Balkan tinder-box." The I.W.W. unfurls its flag and labor begins to rally. William Hohenzollern casts envious eyes at British supremacy on the high seas, and the intense and bitter naval competition between the two nations starts. Suddenly a shot is fired and one bullet in an Archduke's breast is the signal that sets the world in flames.

War is here—and much more than war. Red Revolution in Russia; undeclared war in China; an uprising and Mussolini in Italy; revolution and Hitler in Germany; civil war in Spain; seizures, invasions, and the Axis. And war again.

This is a world in convulsion. A bitter world of disillusionment—but also of reorientation toward change in the very roots of society. The convulsion runs clear through the human fabric, toppling old beliefs, bringing uncertainty. But through it all one certainty emerges: whatever the nature of the future toward which we may be moving, we are apparently completely done with the past. This is reflected clearly in the arts.

Music until recently had been following a well defined, uninterrupted course reaching across three centuries of gradual development. Composers, however daring, moved within the boundaries of certain fundamentals which were accepted as axiomatic. Their harmonies, however dissonant they may have seemed when introduced, were merely extensions of existing harmonies and were still based on the acceptance of a hierarchy of chord relationships derived from the major-minor scales. The means employed for the development of musical ideas were based on certain evolving structures, the fugue, and the sonata, and the symphony. Within these forms climaxes were built up through thematic repetition, acceleration, greater volume, mass effects. The orchestra was conceived as a collaboration among four groups of instruments with the string section as the pivot, the central source of tone. And the orchestral score, when duplicating tones were canceled out, was usually reducible to the four tones, bass, tenor, alto, and soprano, deriving from the misty past of choral writing. In fact orchestral writing was always conceived in terms of these four "voices."

Based squarely on these fundamentals music unfolded through several hundred years. Up to Beethoven, composers were chiefly preoccupied with the perfection of these means; following Beethoven, chiefly with their elaboration. But elaboration could not go on forever. The endpoint of refinement was reached in Debussy.

This ultra refinement marked the beginning of a wholesale dissolution of the old rather than the introduction, as Debussy's contemporaries thought, of something new. For although Debussy expressed the ultimate in Romanticism, he abandoned many of the traditional means heretofore employed. In his music we meet the first extensive disregard of the major-minor scales for which he substitutes the wholetone

[109]

scale. His orchestra is no longer a collaboration between four groups of instruments; it is a mingling of individual instruments. His speech is not clear-cut and bold. It is a language of unpronounced emotion, a tonal radiation which hints but never states. And his climaxes are not tremendous clashes of massed tone; they are periods of fading, of extinction.

Stimulated by these departures from the traditional, composers are led to re-evaluate their tools. They search for new and different fundamentals; experiment in this direction and in that; fling frightening new words around—expressionism and polyrhythm, neo-classicism and atonality.

Trying to get away from major-minor harmony, Milhaud experiments with polytonality, combining melodies in different keys. Stravinsky brings in polyrhythms, using his orchestra to express movement rather than emotion and taking as his point of reference not the song but the dance. Thus his music is built upon changing rhythms that constantly fluctuate and intermingle. In the expression of this dynamism of motion, the singing violins not only lose their pivotal place in the orchestra but are sometimes completely absent, as in the introduction to the *Rites of Spring*. Another musical explorer is Schönberg who uses recurring patterns as themes and who adopts a telegraphic, shorthand style. He also introduces atonality, conceiving all twelve tones that lie within the octave as independent harmonic centers, the centers of a twelve-tone chromatic scale.

Much of this new music is conceived as an intermingling of different individual melodies, each moving according to its own laws. From this arises a good deal of dissonance, but neither consonance nor dissonance is deliberately sought for its own sake. However, through the 1920's experimentation runs riot, and it extends in all directions. Composers play around with the jazz idiom. They introduce steam whistles and hammers and alarm clocks and other strange paraphernalia into the orchestra. Attempts are even made to use a phonograph in order to join the voices of the canary and the nightingale to those of the oboe and the flute.

The public, preferring a more sentimental and familiar diet, chafes under these new trends and is bewildered both by the dissonance and the impersonality of much of today's music. It leaves the concert hall unmoved and unconvinced. Indeed, contemporary music has a greater struggle for acceptance than any music of the past. For the composers of today are not merely adding unfamiliar words to an existing language, which is what Debussy and Wagner and other "dangerous radicals" did in the past. They are evolving an entirely new language, and the transition to this new language is as slow and painful as the social and economic readjustment now convulsing the entire world. It is an interesting commentary that in some quarters, where art is regimented, (see pages 158 & 164) these new trends are held too extreme for governmental sanction. Germany, for instance, considers them anarchistic, and Russia finds them formalistic and out of touch with life.

Meantime the status of music also has entered a new phase. For the first time the dominance of opera has been displaced by instrumental music. The cultural importance of the orchestra to the community has been recognized. In Europe the orchestra has achieved the status of a municipally supported institution, and in the United States a tremendous growth in privately endowed new organizations, over 200 since 1900, has taken place.

Another development of great importance has been the rise of the conductor. Just as the 17th and 18th centuries were dominated by the operatic singer, and the 19th century by the instrumental virtuoso, pianist and violinist, so the 20th century is dominated by the conductor. He is today the star performer who plays upon the orchestra as on an instrument of infinite expressive range. Crowds are drawn as much by his personality and interpretative genius as by the music which is played.

Of greatest significance to the future of music has been the development of radio and phonograph. Music has for the first time become democratized, as increasing millions listen at home to the best orchestras and best performers in the world.

As we enter the 1940's, the era of extravagant experimentation has subsided and a dominant trend has emerged. Composers are finding a common ground for the music of the future. This music must be simple and direct. It must be stripped of non-essentials and of padding. It must be international and neo-classic in spirit, akin to music of the 18th century with its small chamber orchestra, its freshness, its clarity, and its emotion held in check. Along with this comes a renewed interest in old instruments, the lute and the harpsichord, and the revival of old music. For composers are overcoming their long and violent reaction against all emotion, and a softening mood has entered music. Awaiting the emergence of a better world, and meantime pressing vigorously forward, especially in the New World (see page 170) the art stands ready to sum up.

RAGTIME SPREADS FROM U.S.A.

OTHER EVENTS: Commonwealth of Australia extends suffrage to women. Joseph Conrad's "Youth" first story to attract attention in a "wider sphere." Reflecting new feminine freedoms, U. S. women discard sidesaddle; adopt rouge and bridge. In Paris Debussy's "Pelléas and Mélisande" is a popular success. Russia suppresses revolting peasants; jails young revolutionary, Stalin. Tsetse fly brings wholesale death to Uganda natives. Delius composes . . .

APPALACHIA; VARIATIONS ON AN OLD SLAVE SONG (SEE PAGE 184).

Only in recent years has the music of Delius reached out beyond a narrow circle of admirers. There are many reasons for this neglect.

Delius was born in England, yet he began his musical career in the United States, and later settled in a quiet suburb near Paris. English musicians were therefore slow to claim him as their own, especially since he was largely self-educated and neither taught, performed nor otherwise "belonged" to the profession. All Europe, meantime was swept up by Debussy, and though the impressionism of Delius was more subtle and of far greater sweep than Debussy's, it lacked the buoyant quality found in the Frenchman's music and was eclipsed by it. For years Germany was the only country that gave Delius a sympathetic audience. Indeed, it took a German, Bernard van Dieren, to point out to the British Delius' "essential Englishness."

Delius has left a great deal of varied and exceedingly fine music; the lyrically passionate *Sea Drift;* the epic *Mass of Life;* the sombre but glowing *Paris;* the pastoral *Brigg Fair.* In his orchestral-choral *Appalachia* he has recreated the poignant mood of "longing melancholy and childlike humor" associated with the great Mississippi of the plantation days. "Appalachia," a note prefixed to the orchestral score informs us "is an old Indian name for North America."

FIRST MOVIE
GREAT TRAIN ROBBERY

OTHER EVENTS: Wright Brothers make first successful airplane flight; press, skeptical, refuses to take notice until 1908. Japanese Admiral Togo destroys Russia's fleet. "Fantastic," says world of science of Einstein's Theory of Relativity. An Italian tenor, Caruso, begins Metropolitan Opera season. England raises speed limit to 20 m.p.h. Binet, in France, introduces intelligence tests. Paris decrees "fin de siecle" fashions. Debussy composes . . .

LA MER;—"THE SEA"—(SEE PAGE 183).

Since Debussy derived his impressionism from the poets who, in turn, took over the idea from the painters, it is reasonable to assume that the essential characteristics of his art would have remained the same irrespective of the medium he employed. Thinking of Debussy in these terms—as a painter in tone—therefore throws light on certain differences between his music and that of his predecessors such as Felix Mendelssohn.

[116]

If Mendelssohn and Debussy had left on canvas a record of, let us say, a railroad station, the differences in their approach would have been easy to point out. Mendelssohn would doubtless have revealed the busy scene with utmost clarity—the train, the glistening locomotive, the postures, gestures, and expressions of the bustling passengers, down to the last detail. Debussy would have merely suggested the same scene. He would have shown a few indistinct scurrying figures, the locomotive half-hidden in a pall of smoke, perhaps part of the high, vaulted ceiling, to add a touch of spaciousness.

From the epic *La Mer*, presenting three different aspects of the sea, to the simplest piano piece, Debussy invites the listener to fill in through personal reminiscence and association the details of what he is conveying. This is the reason why his music is elusive and must be met more than half-way if it is to reveal its fascination.

C. S. ROLLS & F. H. ROYCE MERGED

OTHER EVENTS: Swiss Simplon Tunnel, longest in world (121/4 miles) opened to traffic. "Strange, pungent odor" in stockyards described in Upton Sinclair's "The Jungle" shocks U. S. public into supporting Pure Food Legislation. Wassermann develops famous test. Guarded discussion of venereal diseases in Ladies' Home Journal unleashes furious protests. Zeppelin's airship makes 1st successful flight. Quake and fire devastate San Francisco. Liadov composes

EIGHT RUSSIAN FOLKSONGS; OP. 58 (SEE PAGE 193).

Liadov has been justly called the wizard of fairy tale and folksong in Russian music. Although his slender art could not stand competition with the more robust treatment of similar material by his teacher, Rimsky-Korsakoff, his was a magic touch of which the older master was incapable.

A shy, unprepossessing man, Liadov shunned the crowd, avoided even old acquaintances. He

Anatol Liadov

came to life only in the privacy of his quiet, comfortable study where he abandoned himself freely to the inspiration of a legendary, pagan world of fancy.

To Liadov, such images as the proud falcon on the alder tree, bewailing a deep sorrow; the snows which, while blanketing the world, had failed to cover the maiden's sorrow; the enchanted doves steering their flight toward the cradle of the peasant child—were real. They were more real than life, and they evoked from Liadov a radiant light that tingled his imagination, releasing his poetic powers.

Immersed as Liadov was in visions from this world of fancy, it is but natural that he should have produced what is perhaps the most convincing symphonic setting of the Russian folksong—eight gems of vivid sensitive tone painting. He left three other delicate orchestral works; *Baba Yaga, Kikimora,* and *The Enchanted Lake.*

TSAR'S UKASE DISSOLVES DUMA

OTHER EVENTS: Cullinan Diamond, 3 times size of any known stone (3025 car.) Transvaal's gift to Edward VII. Liner Lusitania makes maiden voyage to N. Y. (5d. 11½ h.). First Ziegfeld Follies a smash hit. "Degrading," declare Met. Opera patrons forcing withdrawal of R. Strauss' "Salome." Arrival of 1,285,000 new European immigrants begins to crowd U. S. melting pot. Voting in Russia further restricted by new repressive laws. Rachmaninoff composes . . .

THE ISLE OF THE DEAD; SYMPHONIC POEM, OP. 29 (SEE PAGE 198).

A man of deep emotion and great sincerity, Sergei Rachmaninoff has endured the pain that comes from being stalked persistently by cruel and frustrating circumstance. A musician of exceptional gifts, he has for years been dwarfed as a composer by his own prodigious talents as a pianist. A Romanticist and a conservative, holding on doggedly to the past, he has nevertheless lived on to witness music running into channels with which he has no common bond, and the world changing to noisy speed and mass production for which he has no feeling and no sympathy.

Finally, though a Russian by birth, by choice, by temperament, indeed, through every breath he draws, Rachmaninoff has found himself turned loose upon the world to live the life of a political exile, his music condemned and banned as decadent by his own countrymen. Smiling but wounded deeply, Rachmaninoff has withdrawn into himself, composing little and seeing practically no one.

Meanwhile, with each succeeding year, his music has been gaining in prestige and popularity. His *Second Symphony* and *Second Piano Concerto* are in the repertoire of most orchestras. His songs are featured at recitals. And his *Isle of the Dead,* inspired by Böcklin's famous painting, has been declared unique—a masterpiece of dark splendor and exalted majesty.

PICASSO FOUNDS CUBISM

OTHER EVENTS: Huge meteor lands in Siberia; crash heard 400 miles away. Belgium annexes the Congo; Ghandi reported a stretcher-bearer in British suppression of Natal insurrection. "Will ladies revolt?" asks N. Y. Times as city passes ordinance making smoking illegal. Red Cross sells first Xmas seals. First G-men organized. "Why so long?" critics query of Bennett's "Old Wives Tale." Tolstoy celebrates 80th anniversary. Scriabin composes . . .

POEM OF ECSTASY (SEE PAGE 203).

Genius, mystic, fanatic, Alexander Scriabin stirred up a tremendous uproar when he appeared in the world of music, some holding him to be a fake, others insisting that he was the greatest of living musicians. Rimsky-Korsakoff was the most gentle and tactful when he characterized Scriabin as "somewhat warped and self-opinionated." The Russian critic Sabaneyev referred to him less kindly as a "megalomaniac whose conviction in his own divineness was complete;" and the British critic Cecil Gray dismissed him tersely as "the giant crocodile of modern music."

The uproar had its origin in the fact that Scriabin, brilliant pianist and composer though he was, was born with a philosophical bee in his bonnet. Not content with writing music for others to enjoy as music, he conceived his compositions as means of conveying religious experience. And, though essentially a miniaturist whose instrument was the piano, he carried this "mission" over to the wider vistas of orchestral writing.

The "Poem of Fire" *Prometheus,* and the acrid *Poem of Ecstasy,* are his two most ambitious works; and each is best approached on its own level. For as Paul Rosenfeld reminds us, these works "were conceived as rituals. They were planned as ceremonies of deification by ecstasy in which performers and auditors engaged as active and passive celebrants."

PEARY REACHES NORTH POLE

OTHER EVENTS: Famous "tin Lizzie" T-model Ford rolls off the assembly line. Bleriot first to fly across English Channel. "Subversive!" says Russian censor barring Rimsky's "Coq d'Or" from the stage. Three suffragettes chain themselves to statue in Br. Parliament. Pundits discourse on expressionist trends in music; general public more concerned with century's first short skirts. W. H. Taft, first golf-playing President, inaugurated. Mahler composes . . .

DAS LIED VON DER ERDE;—"THE SONG OF THE EARTH"—(SEE PAGE 194).

The Viennese composer Mahler has been called the greatest failure in music, a mere "silhouette of a great man." This is undoubtedly too harsh a judgment, though it is clear that Mahler, with all his talent, fell far short of his ideas. Like Scriabin, he sought to give expression to experiences of a scope and subtlety out of all proportion to his creative powers. Like Bruckner, with whom his name is closely linked both as a friend and pupil, he aroused heated discussion which came to nothing since his music had fared badly and is, in fact, largely unknown except to a small group of faithful devotees.

A "classical Romanticist," intense, dynamic, mystic, superstitious, acclaimed as a great conductor, Mahler sought to win equal recognition in the field of composition. He wrote eight huge symphonies of vehement, exalted music. When he came to the ninth, he balked (recalling that the Ninth was Beethoven's last) and called it a song cycle. This hauntingly nostalgic *Song of the Earth,* a musical setting of a Chinese 8th century poem, is really a symphony with voices in all but name. Of this work, which is undoubtedly Mahler's best, Arnold Schönberg has said that it "conveys an almost passionless embodiment of beauty, perceptible only to those who can renounce animal warmth and feel at home in the coolness of the spirit."

MOUNT ETNA ERUPTS

OTHER EVENTS: Reign of George V begins. In celebration, the earth whirls through tail of Halley's comet; fearing end of world many hide in basements, cyclone cellars. Japan annexes Korea. Helen Keller, famous blind-deaf-mute, writes "The World I Live In." Union of So. Africa formed. U. S. Govt. starts collecting Indian melodies with aid of phonograph. Ragtime rage reaches peak in Berlin's "Alexander's Ragtime Band." Schönberg composes . . .

GURRE-LIEDER (SEE PAGE 201).

Wild, futuristic, wilfully ugly, hideous, coldly cerebral, unmusical—these are but some of the adjectives that have been hurled at Schönberg's music. Probably no other composer has ever had to face more hostile and tumultuous audiences or more antagonistic critics. No other living composer occupies a more enigmatic position, for in spite of its universality, the significance of Schönberg's music is far from clarified. What we do know is that Schönberg has been remarkably honest with himself and fearless in his dealings with the world, and that his progress into the musical unknown has been a matter not of choice but of artistic necessity.

Born in Vienna, poor, largely self-taught, but irresistibly drawn to music, Schönberg started out humbly. To make a living he free-lanced as an orchestrator, scoring 6000 pages of light music between 1901–11, thus delaying the completion of the *Gurre-Songs* (so named because the work deals with the tribulations of the Danish King Waldemar at his castle of Gurre). Even while working on this mammoth, ultra-Romantic piece, Schönberg grew dissatisfied, and, aboutfacing, he slowly worked his way into a new musical idiom, created by himself. In his *Five Orchestral Pieces, Pierrot Lunaire,* etc., he adopted a language terse, aphoristic, based on a new concept of harmony, thus introducing what has been aptly described as "a new dimention in music."

TRANSATLANTIC CHESS MATCH BY CABLE

OTHER EVENTS: Pandemonium reigns at the Louvre over mysterious theft of da Vinci's "Mona Lisa." "Knocks over admirals like nine-pins," is press report as Winston Churchill called to the Admiralty to put fleet on the alert. England is 1st country to introduce compulsory unemployment insurance nationally. Amundsen reaches South Pole in race with Scott. Parachute jumping is in the news. Heyday of the player piano fast approaching. Stravinsky composes . . .

PETROUCHKA; SUITE (SEE PAGE 206).

In three successive years with three successive works, all three of them ballets—*The Fire Bird, Petrouchka,* and the *Rite of Spring*—Stravinsky shook music inside out and settled over it as the most spectacular figure of his time.

In the first of these works, though still leaning on a vocabulary acquired from his teacher, Rimsky-Korsakoff, Stravinsky revealed for the first time his strikingly original turn of mind.

Igor Stravinsky

With *Petrouchka* he clinched his international reputation by eliciting from the orchestra a whole new set of tonal values—sounds suggestive of the atmosphere of a Russian country fair—a festive, gaudy, boisterous bedlam pierced by brazen street-song tunes. With the third work, the *Rite of Spring (Le Sacre du Printemps)*, which deals with the worship of the forces of Nature by primitive man, Stravinsky precipitated a riot. Never before had music of such terrifying vehemence been heard, and never did a single work impress itself so deeply on its time.

In later years Stravinsky has shown steadily increasing powers as a technician and a continuous growth which finally has carried him over into the neo-classical camp. However, he never has equalled his three early works—three lonely masterpieces which mark an era and label Stravinsky as one of the most dynamic composers of the 20th century.

TITANIC DISASTER

OTHER EVENTS: Imperial "Yellow Dragon" lowered at British legation as China becomes a republic. First blues (Memphis) published in U. S. "Must not reach France," says Clemenceau of Albanian outbreak of cholera. Gestalt psychology, in Germany, claims personality not an addition of traits. Workmen's insurance introduced in Russia. Arizona, New Mexico are latest U. S. States; Wilson, new U. S. President; Hitler a carpenter in Munich. Ravel orchestrates . . .

PAVANE FOR A DEAD INFANTA; ORIGINALLY FOR PIANO, 1899 (SEE PAGE 199).

Small, thin, neat, graying, laconic, inconspicuous in a crowd of admirers thronging backstage to offer their respects after he had finished playing, Maurice Ravel toward the end of his career could easily have been mistaken for an obscure actor, a retired music critic—anything but the eminent composer that he was—one of the most distinguished and most gifted men of France.

Yet in listening to Ravel's music, the qualities that had slowly brought him to the top could hardly pass unnoticed; his polish, clarity, restraint, orderliness, asceticism, and subtle irony —all of them characteristics that have so clearly differentiated Ravel's music from the warmer and more nebulous impressionism of Claude Debussy.

Ravel was a fastidious worker, a real craftsman, a consummate master of orchestration. He was also a pianist, though not a very good one, and was in the habit of conceiving his compositions first as piano pieces which, when the spirit moved him, he re-worked for the orchestra—not just transferring the music to the orchestra but conceiving it, as it were, anew. Through this recreative process passed some of his most original compositions, among them the *Pavane,* a charming early work, tender and luminous in its veiled sadness and its detachment from earthly care.

PEACE PALACE, THE HAGUE, DEDICATED

OTHER EVENTS: U. S. starts Parcel Post service. Disapproving audience riots at Paris premiere of Stravinsky's "Rite of Spring." Atom structure discovered by Bohn, Danish scientist. ". . . has small regard for conventional morality," says N. Y. Times of Lawrence's "Sons and Lovers." A wave of ordinances, banning unprotected women's hatpins, sweeps world. 16th Amendment brings U. S. Federal income tax. Chaplin steps into pictures. Sibelius composes . . .

THE BARD; TONE POEM (SEE PAGE 204).

The highly individual and strongly nationalistic Sibelius has been called "an almost incredible apparition in contemporaneous music." For in his calm, unhurried way Sibelius, sturdy son of Finland that he is, has followed his artistic destiny heedless of public taste, unmindful of current trends and fashions, undaunted by the neglect which he endured for many years. For only in Finland was he recognized at once.

Jean Sibelius

In the folk legends of his country, Sibelius
sought his inspiration; from his austere Northern environment he drew his strength. These
he expressed in music that is evocative and
darkly brooding. The impact of this music is
often directly overwhelming; almost elemental,
but its power may also lie in its restraint. This
we are made to realize when listening to *The
Bard* which is among Sibelius' best though least
known shorter works. The bard, we sense . . .

". . . converses with the spirits of the de-
parted; with motionless and silent clouds. The
cold moonlight sheds its faint lustre on his head;
the fox peeps out of the ruined tower; the
thistle shakes its beard . . . and the strings of
the harp, as the hand of age, as the tale of
other times, sigh and rustle in the winter's
wind."

In this short passage, written long ago, William Hazlitt gives us the mood and the essential
spirit of the work.

SUFFRAGETTES RIOT IN ENGLAND

OTHER EVENTS: King George V in state-ment "approves" of boxing. Switzerland embar-rassed as invitation to Panama Canal opening asks navy's participation. Sarajevo murder in mid-summer causes ripple of apprehension. People scan newspapers as Tsar receives Russian leaders; orders lights out in the Baltic. "Now or never," is Kaiser's comment. Press reports 1st shots in World War I. Cirey, France, overwhelmed. Sun in total eclipse. Vaughan Williams composes.

A LONDON SYMPHONY (SEE PAGE 208).

Following Handel's triumphs in 18th century Britain, English music suffered a decline. Na-tive composers, dazzled by the success of this amazing "foreigner" (or squelched by him if they showed too much promise) turned their attention from the homeland and began imitat-ing German and Italian styles—but with so little consequence that they achieved not one out-standing work in the century and a half that followed.

Ralph Vaughan Williams

During the latter part of the 19th century, England produced Elgar, Sullivan, and Delius. Yet, theirs was not a distinctly native form of art, and music nourished directly from the soil did not reassert itself in earnest until, roughly, 1904—the year when a young clergyman's son joined the English Folk-Song Society and started diligently scouring Norfolk for old country tunes. This young man, whose subsequent activities as a composer and teacher heralded the appearance of a group of composers producing music thoroughly native to England, was Vaughan Williams.

The composer of *A London Symphony*, or "A Symphony by a Londoner," as he would have it, is so wholly English that the appeal of his music depends to some extent on the possession by the listener of a common bond with Britain. And heartening music it is for those who feel with it, spun of homely robustness, yet always varied and poetic.

NOBEL PEACE PRIZE UNCLAIMED

OTHER EVENTS: Poison gas appears in Europe's war. Margaret Sanger faces Federal indictment in fight for birth control; "A peril to civilization," N. J. churchman declares. Report that Henry Ford's "peace mission" may stop hostilities sends Am. Tobacco stocks tumbling. Jazz from New Orleans transplanted to Chicago. "Science and Health" shows increased sales; is included in U. S. mail order catalogs. Lusitania sinking protested. Falla composes . . .

NIGHTS IN THE GARDENS OF SPAIN,
FOR PIANO AND ORCHESTRA (SEE PAGE 185).

In Spain as in England, Nationalism in music was late in coming. When it appeared and flowered in the works of Albeniz, Granados, Turina, Falla, music was enriched by an art both colorful and vital.

The most eminent of the Spanish nationalists is Falla. His music has all the swift and restless passion, all the suppressed excitement of the Andalusian folksong; yet all his thoughts are touched with clarity and an aristocratic polish.

When writing for the orchestra, Falla leans heavily on the piano to give his music its incisive sharpness, and on the woodwinds, especially the oboe, to impart to it its sensuous savor. Yet Falla is never showy or vulgar, for of all composers now writing music he is perhaps the most poetic and most sensitive.

When he was writing his three nocturnes, *Nights in the Gardens of Spain,* Falla lived in Paris and knew many an anguished hour for lack of nourishment. He never forgot it. In later years, no longer strained financially, he came to occupy a comfortable little house perched on a hillside outside Granada. And every morning he walked down through his tiny garden and out into the city that lies below, carrying a basket filled with food. The poor of Granada learned to watch for his trim, diminutive figure; and they came to know and love him for his discreet words of cheer and tender kindness.

DAYLIGHT SAVING IN ENGLAND

OTHER EVENTS: British try out tanks on Western Front. Berlin calls them trifling; restricts actors' purchase of new costumes. "Mr. Britling sees it through" by H. G. Wells called a buttress to morale. Swept by slogan "he kept us out of war" U. S. reelects Wilson. Battles of Verdun and Jutland indecisive. Mooney sentenced in San Francisco explosion. Turks are jubilant as Dardanelles hold, defying Allies. Bloch composes . . .

SCHELOMO; HEBREW RHAPSODY FOR CELLO AND ORCHESTRA (SEE PAGE 179).

In the past Jewish composers seeking world-wide recognition have largely ignored their Jewish heritage, expressing themselves in a Germanic or Latin style. Now, for the first time in the troubled history of the Jewish people, a composer has come forward not to subordinate his Judaism but to proclaim it for the whole world to hear.

This composer, the son of a clock maker, was

born in Switzerland. At twelve he made this pledge, to be a Jew in music, wrote down his resolution on a scrap of paper, and solemnly burned it on a pile of stones. During the years that followed, he never forgot this pledge. For most of his outstanding works, the *Israel* Symphony, The *Three Jewish Poems*, and the rhapsody which bears the name of the illustrious King Solomon, he sought his inspiration in Hebraic lore and found it there.

In *Schelomo*, Bloch explains, he has set forth the Jewish love of justice; the sorrow and immensity of the Book of Job; the frank sensuality and subtle eloquence of the Song of Songs. He need not have explained. The Hebraic character of the rhapsody is apparent from its first ardent measures. This rich, impassioned music is permeated, as Guido Pannain has said, "by a sense of isolation of the Jewish soul in the universe, conscious of its destiny—to wait while wandering."

MATA HARI, SPY, EXECUTED BY FRENCH

OTHER EVENTS: Birth rate in warring nations reported dropping. "I'd like to buy a farm in England," says the Tsar, abdicating, as revolution sweeps Russia. U. S. joins Allies in war on Germany. Rumors spread of mutiny in French army. "A propagandist!" cries Saint-Saëns pointing finger at Wagner's works. Mutiny in German fleet confirmed. Typewriter makes inconspicuous debut as orchestral instrument. Soviets seize power in Russia. Prokofieff composes . . .

SYMPHONY IN D MAJOR, OP. 25—"CLASSICAL"—(SEE PAGE 197).

Nineteen hundred seventeen was Russia's year of turmoil: revolution in March against the old regime; uprisings in midsummer; continued unrest and revolution in November, displacing the liberals who had displaced the Tsar. During this year of social stress Serge Prokofieff, though following closely every move of the unfolding drama, kept up his schedule as best he could and finally completed his answer to the critics who had for years harassed him for writing what they described as diabolically brutal music.

Deftly, and with a twinkle in his eye, Prokofieff confounded his tormentors by presenting them with the *"Classical" Symphony*—an impish, teasing work, acrid in flavor but written in accord with the best classical tradition and in its way as polished as anything from the pen of Haydn or Mozart.

Today this is old history. Prokofieff has long since "arrived." He stands in the vanguard of contemporary music, a many-sided and sophisticated personality. As a composer he has displayed boundless vitality and great enterprise, turning out work after work. Many of these have been outstanding; many have been well liked and have been frequently performed; yet none has attracted a following as wide or enthusiastic as has the youthful, impudently graceful *"Classical" Symphony*, composed a quarter of a century ago.

MUSSOLINI
MARCHES
ON ROME

OTHER EVENTS: Famine grips Russia. Bootleggers rise to the occasion as prohibition blankets the U. S. First airplane to cross Atlantic; 2nd year of radio broadcasting; 13th edition of Wells' "Outline of History." People say: How's your sex life? read Lewis' "Babbitt"; dance the Charleston. Kemal Pasha proclaims Turkish Republic. Readers Digest is launched. Low waistline and bobbed hair usher in age of the flapper. Ibert composes . . .

ESCALES;—"PORTS OF CALL"—(SEE PAGE 192).

"In whatever Jaques Ibert presents to his hearers," writes Andre George, "there is clarity and good quality and the impression of a work well done." But the qualities of this French composer that are perhaps most ingratiating are his youthfulness of spirit and his typically Gallic wit.

Already as a youngster Ibert gave evidence of this, for of all the people he ever met at his father's home, the little man in authority—

pretentious in manner, solemn in expression—
seemed to him the funniest. Gifted, versatile,
imaginative—but untutored—Ibert when he was
only twenty-nine had the temerity to apply for
the *Prix de Rome*, famed musicians' laurel, without troubling first to avail himself of the tutelage
of the Paris Conservatory. To the dismay of
the academicians and in spite of their objections,
he received the award.

One of the first works to come from his pen
after this victory was the suite *Escale*, a fantasy
on three tunes—a calm Italian melody, a melancholy phrase from Tunis, a Moorish refrain
from the coast of Spain—overheard while on a
cruise in the Mediterranean. The work was immediately successful. Indeed, there is an
abundance of riches in this imaginative piece—
vigor and colorful orchestration and a peculiarly
veiled poetic quality, akin to Debussy's yet somehow much closer in spirit to our own day than
the impressionism of the older master.

JAPANESE EARTHQUAKE KILLS ½ MILLION

OTHER EVENTS: German labor unions report membership drop. Paris police stop jazz band at funeral; relatives insist dead man's desire. Hitler's beer-hall "putsch" fails. French and Belgians occupy the Ruhr. "Jazz will live as art," Paul Whiteman quoted declaring. "Unbending," says Baltimore Sun of Calvin Coolidge, new U. S. President. "Yes, we have no bananas," hit tune of the moment. Time Magazine begins to march. Milhaud composes . . .

THE CREATION OF THE WORLD; A NEGRO BALLET (SEE PAGE 195).

In February 1924 at Carnegie Hall, Paul Whiteman introduced George Gershwin's *Rhapsody in Blue*, a composition which was at once hailed as a masterpiece. Ever since that historic concert, Gershwin has been regarded as the first composer to have succeeded in producing symphonic jazz.

To keep the record straight, and without any thought of belittling Gershwin's accomplishment, it should be brought to the attention of the music lover that the first masterpiece of symphonic jazz was written not by Gershwin but by a Frenchman, and that it was produced not at Carnegie Hall, New York, in 1924 but a year earlier in Paris. This composition, the work of Darius Milhaud, is *The Creation of the World,* a Negro ballet based on an African legend of the Creation.

In this short work, Milhaud, who is a leading French composer of extremist tendencies (see page 110), has used the more elemental Harlem, rather than the more elegant Broadway idiom employed by Gershwin. His music is therefore less dashing and spectacular than the *Rhapsody,* but it is just as eloquent and vital in a different way. Experts who have given the matter study have said that it embodies "the quintessence of the Negro style;" and anyone who listens to it sympathetically will hardly disagree with them, for the *Creation* is a fascinating piece of music.

SPEAKEASY ERA AT PEAK

OTHER EVENTS: Woodrow Wilson and Lenin die within two weeks of each other. Tennessee accepts W. J. Bryan's testimony that world was created in 4404 B.C.; bans teaching of evolution in schools. Of experimental talkies Edison says: "Americans don't want them." Mexico nationalizes church property. Women riot at bier of Valentino, screen idol. Hitler's "Mein Kampf" appears in German (but few take heed). Radiophone spans the Atlantic. Kodaly composes . . .

HÁRY JÁNOS; SUITE FOR ORCHESTRA (SEE PAGE 192).

As the son of a Hungarian stationmaster, Kodály spent his childhood in small, provincial Kecskemét. There every morning and every night he watched and listened as trainloads of singing peasants rolled by the tiny station. These early musical impressions affected Kodály profoundly. They aroused in him the ardent wish to know the music of his people and led him to travel throughout the countryside

Zoltan Kodály

collecting and studying Hungarian folksong.

Doubtless because of this intensive study, Kodály's music is permeated with a robust freshness and directness unmistakably national in spirit. It is Hungarian through and through; and it is music of the highest order. For Kodály has composed sparingly, giving a great deal of thought and care to the execution of each composition.

His major work is the opera *Háry János*. It tells of the exploits of Háry, an ex-soldier, who on returning home regales a group of gaping peasants with a recital of his experiences in the army. Carried away by his own eloquence, Háry tells of his countless feats of valor, his lurid love affairs, his hand-to-hand encounter with the Emperor Napoleon (to whom, so Háry boasts, he for good measure administered a kick). This opera is to the Hungarians what Smetana's *Bartered Bride* is to the Czechs. As a concert suite it has enjoyed great popularity.

LINDBERGH FLIES NON-STOP N.Y. TO PARIS

OTHER EVENTS: Levees crumble in disastrous Mississippi flood. Economists warn of impending collapse of German economic system. "Vulgar music to be investigated," says Berlin Govt. of sudden craze for U. S. vocal jazz. Celebrated case is closed as Sacco and Vanzetti executed. "Only in war does man attain highest ideal," proclaims Mussolini. Russian crown jewels turn up at London auction. Chiang Kai-Chek called China's hope. Respighi composes.

GLI UCELLI;—"THE BIRDS"—SUITE FOR ORCHESTRA (SEE PAGE 199).

Throughout his life Respighi remained at odds with the two major influences of his youth. When at nine he enrolled at the Musical Lyceum at Bologna, he fell into the hands of two excellent Italian teachers who by conviction were Classicists, resisting with dogged conscientiousness any concession to the picturesque. When, later, he traveled across Europe to St. Petersburg to place himself in the hands of the Russian wizard of the orchestra, Rimsky-Korsakoff, he found himself steered just as firmly in the opposite direction.

A nature more vitally endowed would have integrated both influences, but Respighi, himself half Romanticist, half Classicist, never made up his mind which muse to woo. Much of his music, though very colorful and varied and poetic, is seldom more than an attempt to please. However, his ironic bent, and flair for orchestration resulted in several compositions of true merit—none as delightful as the little suite in which he paid tribute to creatures endowed with the greatest musical gifts—birds. In this suite Respeghi combined several little pieces originally written by various 17th and 18th century composers, and scored them ingeniously, producing a work modern in garb yet quaintly old in spirit—music utterly enjoyable in its sly humor, its lack of artifice, and its disarming semblance of complete simplicity.

1927

PORTUGAL BANS WALKING BAREFOOT

OTHER EVENTS: Nations forswear war in Kellogg-Briand Pact. Millions spent on Hollywood's first talkies; people complain they hurt their ears. Turkey adopts Latin alphabet. Britain passes women's suffrage; lady M. P.'s declare they want enlarged lounge rooms. In a garage 12 people labor over "Steamboat Willie," 1st Mickey Mouse. Year of prosperity ends in Wall Street crash. Spengler's "Decline of the West" is food for thought. Walton composes . . .

CONCERTO FOR VIOLA AND ORCHESTRA (SEE PAGE 210).

Although the name William Walton is a familiar one to British concert goers, many Americans are still unaware of its existence. Unaccountably, England is still thought of by many over here as a country which is musically sterile. We grant the British their Purcell, but we insist that as a people they are decidedly unmusical—perhaps forgetting, sometimes not realizing that Vaughan Williams has given us his

London and *Pastoral* symphonies, and Bliss his *Music for Strings,* and Walton his eloquent *Concerto.*

Walton, who is today considered "the white hope of British music," received his early training from his father, a music teacher. He then became a chorister at Christ Church Cathedral, Oxford. In 1923 he had a string quartet performed. It was characterized as "horrible." However, within three years, Walton was scoring a spectacular success with his satyrical *Facade.* Three more years, and his rhapsodic *Viola Concerto* was being given its premiere in London with Paul Hindemith as soloist.

Most music critics, when speaking of contemporary music, find it prudent to hold their enthusiasm in check. Yet even conservative Donald Tovey exclaimed when he heard Walton's *Concerto:* "I can see no limit to the tone-poet who created it." Many people have since had occasion to agree with him.

FRENCH START
MAGINOT LINE

OTHER EVENTS: Ethiopia's Haile Selassie declares himself Emperor; is congratulated by Pres. Hoover. Berlin applauds Milhaud's opera "Chr. Columbus" which uses movies to reveal thoughts of stage characters. Unemployed in U. S. sell apples in streets; rumba is latest dance craze. Word from Washington: "Prosperity just around the corner"; N. Y. Times editorial: "Cautious Hope." Basic English is latest attempt at an international language. Hanson composes . . .

SYMPHONY NO. 2, OP. 30;—"ROMANTIC"—

(SEE PAGE 190).

Affable, entertaining, and well disposed to venture an opinion on almost any subject, Howard Hanson, energetic director of the Eastman School of Music, can be relied upon to furnish good "news copy;" and the reporters love to interview him.

Born of Swedish parents at Wahoo, Nebraska, Hanson came to New York as a youth to study music at the Institute of Musical Art. At 19 he was already teaching on the Pacific Coast. At 25 he went to study in Rome. Since his return he has been active not merely as a composer but as an educator, encouraging native talent.

In 1930 Hanson was commissioned to compose a work for performance at the fiftieth anniversary of the Boston Symphony Orchestra. He wrote a symphony which he called *"Romantic"* because he wanted it to reflect American life, and most Americans, he thought, in spite of their boasted industrialization, are incurable romantics. When pressed for a more specific statement about this music which by its healthy vigor had wrung words of praise even from music critics, Hanson obligingly complied. The work represents, he said, "my escape from a rather bitter type of modern musical realism which occupies so large a place in contemporary thought."

In 1934 Hanson's opera *Merry Mount* was produced at the Metropolitan Opera, New York.

JAZZING OF CLASSICS IN U.S. PROTESTED

OTHER EVENTS: House to house fighting rages in Shanghai as Japan seizes city in undeclared war. U. S. depression hits bottom; 31,822 business failures reported in year. "Doing all we can," says Jersey police in kidnapping of Col. Lindbergh's son. British witness 1st television broadcast. Technocracy, a "panicky theory," flares briefly. Paris fashions feature straight silhouettes. Franklin D. Roosevelt elected President. Villa-Lobos composes . . .

BACHIANA BRASILEIRA NO. 1 FOR EIGHT CELLI (SEE PAGE 209).

When Villa-Lobos, today a leading South American composer, went to Paris as a young Brazilian conductor-pianist, French musicians assumed that this unknown young "rustic" from across the ocean had come to study composition. "I came," he told them, "not to study but to show you what I have done."

This straightforwardness of speech which is spontaneous and completely unselfconscious, is characteristic of Villa-Lobos the man no less than Villa-Lobos the composer. With roots deep in the savage and exotic vastness of the Amazon yet with a vigorously intellectual background, for his father was a humanist-writer and an amateur musician of considerable skill, Villa-Lobos has brought to contemporary music a unique blend of primitiveness and sophistication, welded together by a thorough mastery of Western technique.

Most curious of all for one whose art is steeped in Brazilian folk music, Villa-Lobos worships at the shrine of Johann Sebastian Bach. He believes not only that Bach is the most universal of all geniuses. All life, he thinks, begins and ends in Bach in whose music it is reflected. It is "to express his own relation and that of the art of his people to this German master," that Villa-Lobos composed his Bachiana suites—music characterized by its sober earnestness and great distinction.

REICHSTAG FIRE

OTHER EVENTS: Germany bans use of cosmetics; totalitarian state proclaimed official goal. "Who's afraid of the big bad wolf," is world sensation as Disney releases "Three Little Pigs." Labor govt. in Norway promises stability. A. F. of L. estimates 13 million U. S. unemployed. New York lawyer says popularity of jigsaw puzzle indicates turn to prosperity. Hitler's "Mein Kampf" is a flop in English translation. Chavez composes . . .

SINFONIA DE ANTIGONA (SEE PAGE 181).

In the music of Mexico's Carlos Chavez there is no trace of the tropical opulence that lurks in the background of many of the works of his Brazilian colleague, Villa-Lobos. For his is not an art based on a folk-idiom partly African. Although equally nationalistic, the music of this gifted contemporary composer expresses the different, Amerindian culture of the Mexican peon—more terse and more restrained and yet more savagely intense.

Carlos Chavez

Chavez has for some time been recognized as the most eminent among Mexican composers and has enjoyed an international reputation not merely as a composer but as a revitalizer of Mexico's musical culture. In 1928 he organized the Mexican Symphony Orchestra. In 1933 he was appointed by his government as the Chief of the Department of Fine Arts; and in that year he wrote the *Sinfonia de Antigona,* one of his major works.

This music, written for Jean Cocteau's version of Sophocles' "Antigone" is lean, laconic, and austere. At first hearing it may repel by its impersonality, but this is an impression against which music lovers must be forewarned. "Thereafter," says music critic Olin Downes, "one is seized by the truthfulness, clearness of line, and concentrated expression of the piece. There is something in it, in a quasi-barbaric and Mexican way, that runs parallel to the severity and crudeness of a savage wood carving."

DUST STORMS DEVASTATE U.S. MIDWEST

OTHER EVENTS: Revelations of French Govt. corruption explodes in Paris riots. Leaning Tower of Pisa starts moving north; puzzles observers by turning around and moving south. Turkey abolishes titles; orders officials to learn to operate typewriters. Hitler unleashes "blood purge" of party; is dropped from British Who's Who. In a Canadian log house Dr. Dafoe delivers Dionne Quintuplets. Swing music is latest U. S. enthusiasm. Hindemith composes . . .

SYMPHONY MATHIS DER MALER;—
"MATHIS THE PAINTER"—(SEE PAGE 191).

Nothing else in contemporary art is as expressive of that unhappy gap in human history that separates World War I and World War II as the music of Paul Hindemith. He more than any other artist typifies these years of tension and uncertainty characterized by bitter disillusionment but also by a striving for a new anchorage and a new faith.

Born and schooled in Germany, Hindemith

first came before the public as a viola player. Before long he gained an equally high reputation as a composer and became a leading exponent of "Gebrauchsmusik"—music composed for a specific current need such as use in schools, clubs; movie music, etc.

With the advent of Nazi rule, Hindemith's music was banned for its extremist tendencies as well as for the composer's inclination to "feel at home in Jewish company." The prohibition was so strict that when the eminent conductor, Furtwängler, defied the ban by playing Hindemith's new work *Mathis the Painter,* he was summarily dismissed. This work, originally written as an opera then re-worked as a symphony, deals with the 16th century painter Matthias Gruenewald. The music contained in the Symphony was inspired by three Gruenewald paintings that adorn the Isenhein altar at Colmar: "Angelic Concert;" "Entombment;" and "Temptation of St. Anthony."

HEYDAY
OF CAFE
SOCIETY

OTHER EVENTS: German Jews outlawed; Nazi ritual replaces old school prayers. Fearing neighbor, Switzerland begins to arm. "Home, Sweet Home," sings Oklahoma lawyer to jury defending bank robber client. Will Rogers dies in airplane crash. "Foreign importations must go," says Mussolini; bans crooners from air waves; invades Ethiopia. Persia renamed Iran. Social security, collective bargaining, U. S. laws; "boondogling," U. S. byword. Dohnányi composes . . .

SYMPHONIC MINUTES (SEE PAGE 184).

Hungary today boasts three composers of outstanding talent. Two of these, Béla Bartók (still woefully neglected by the record companies) and Kodály are Nationalists whose music, though contemporary in idiom, rests squarely on Hungarian folksong. The third and oldest of the three, Dohnányi, is distinguished for his infallible good taste and cosmopolitan outlook. He has toured many countries as a pianist, has served as a conductor of several major orchestras, and has by his fine musicianship won general respect.

Leaving the composition of giant works to others, Dohnányi has been satisfied with writing music that is direct and not too deeply probing or intense. Yet so craftsmanlike and polished are his compositions and so filled with poetic feeling that there is scarcely a composer whose music is more gratifying on first acquaintance.

The secret of this warming halo that surrounds Dohnányi's music is simple. He has developed a style compounded of 19th century Romanticism and present-day solidity and terseness. It is this happy combination that makes his four *Symphonic Minutes* such a delightful composition. For here is contemporary music at its best—tuneful and to the point and beautifully orchestrated, without loose ends or rhetoric or cloying sentiment—exactly the thing to play for one's grand aunt and at the same time enjoy oneself.

ROME-BERLIN AXIS

OTHER EVENTS: "Jerusalem Calling," inaugurates ancient city's broadcasting. Soviets publish constitution as Spanish Civil War splits world opinion. Abdicating "to marry the woman I love," says Edward VIII in farewell radio talk. "A false rally," skeptics report of Blum's Popular Front in France. Nazi panzers roll into Rhineland. "Gone With the Wind" makes publishing history. U. S. chemist, R. Williams, succeeds in producing vitamin B_1. Bliss composes . . .

MUSIC FOR STRINGS (SEE PAGE 178).

Of the "younger" British composers, Arthur Bliss is one of the most gifted and outstanding. His music has solidity and independence. Its breezy vigorousness imparts to it a British flavor; its terse expressiveness and moderately acrid dissonance give it a cosmopolitan, fastidious polish.

Bliss is indeed extremely British. Except for a two years sojourn in the United States, where he was married, Bliss has lived almost continuously in England. He studied at the Royal College of Music under Vaughan Williams, served during World War I with the Royal Fusiliers, and is today one of the leading figures in English music.

During the extravagant 1920's, Bliss was regarded as an *enfant terrible* with a vengeance. In 1922 he wrote a daring *"Color" Symphony* in which each movement was inspired by the symbolism of a color—purple suggesting pomp, green standing for hope and youth, etc. When first performed this symphony created a furore, making conservative musicians squirm. Since then, however, Bliss has relaxed into a form of modern Romanticism, and in this mood he has produced several outstanding works. One of these is *Music for Strings*, a composition that is close-knit and stands up well under repeated hearings. Other recent works include, among others: a *Clarinet Quintet*, a *Concerto for Piano and Orchestra*, and the ballet *Checkmate*.

HINDENBURG DISASTER

OTHER EVENTS: Crossing North Pole, Soviet plane flies non-stop Moscow to San Francisco. Versailles Treaty disowned by Hitler. Desertion, cruelty, insanity—legal grounds for divorce, Br. Parliament agrees. ⅓ of U. S. tunes in on Charlie McCarthy. "An epidemic," says press as labor "sits-down" in novel strikes. Tourists flock to Paris Exposition. London jammed for coronation of George VI. Younger generation goes "jitterbug." Shostakovich composes . . .

SYMPHONY NO. 5, OP. 47 (SEE PAGE 203).

Unprecedented in musical history is the career of Dmitri Shostakovich, "composer-laureate of the Soviet state."

Born and brought up on the tide of revolution, Shostakovich fell in quite readily with his country's official view that music should reflect the ideology of communism. At 19 he plunged into composition and produced a string of symphonies (two of them celebrating the Revolution) as well as operas, ballets, and piano and

film music. Of these early works his brilliant
and exciting *First Symphony* was the most successful. Played everywhere, it made him internationally known.

So far everything was going well, but in 1930,
the young composer began to stray from the
ideological path prescribed by communist doctrine. In his music he used satire, flirted with
atonality and other "products of bourgeois
decadence," and this provoked a stinging official
rebuke. Subsequent works aroused further dis-
pleasure, and the composer's music was eventually condemned as formalistic and un-prole-
tarian. Shostakovich, it seemed, faced a crisis in
his career—the imminent possibility of being
"dropped." But as the music world waited in
great suspense, the young composer suddenly
rebounded into official favor. With his dynamic
and eloquent *Fifth Symphony* he scored a triumph and was declared· to be once more at
one with the "realities of the Soviet state."

HURRICANE
STRIKES
NEW ENGLAND

OTHER EVENTS: Hitler takes over Austria. Women adopt upswept hairdo. Chamberlain's "peace for our time" allays war scare; Czechs are victims of appeasement. Liner Queen Mary streaks across Atlantic (3 d. 20 h.). Howard Hughes girdles globe in record time (3 d. 19 h.). Church of England finds Genesis not historical; accepts evolution. "Information, please!" adds sophistication to radio's quiz craze. First news round-up is on the air. Harris composes . . .

SYMPHONY NO. 3 (SEE PAGE 190).

Roy Harris, born in Lincoln County, Oklahoma, has in this symphony expressed something essentially American. Through the music there pulses the spirit of the West, for there is spaciousness here, and vigor boldly uttered, and before us the symphony unfolds a vision of the lonely, wind-swept plains through which the covered wagon pulled its load of hopeful pioneers. According to no less an authority than Dr. Sergei Koussevitzky, this is the first truly great work produced in the United States. The reason for this statement is clear. The music has a certain bleak grandeur, an epic folk quality that rings true. In short, it has real breadth.

Roy Harris has come legitimately by all this. Born of Scotch-Irish parents on the last American frontier, he has crossed broad plains in an oxcart, has earned his living by farming and truck driving, has also studied hard, learning the tools of music here and abroad from the best teachers, achieving recognition as one of the leading "young" progressives in American music. In his *Third Symphony,* he says, he has endeavored to portray a mood of adventure and physical exuberance; of the pathos underlying all human existence; and of the will to power and to action. Recently Harris has surpassed the success even of this symphony by a new "*Folksong*" *Symphony* based on well known American tunes.

NEW YORK WORLD'S FAIR

OTHER EVENTS: Debutantes compete for glamour girl spotlight. "Mein Kampf" in 1st un-expurgated English edition; begins to sell. War scares intensify. Steinbeck's "Grapes of Wrath" tops best-seller list; is ordered burned by E. St. Louis Library. "Non-intervention" bears fruit as Spanish Loyalists surrender. Stratoliners reported in successful tests. Hitler invades Poland. Maginot Line impregnable, experts agree. The word "blitz" ends an era. Gould composes . . .

FOSTER GALLERY (SEE PAGE 188).

Stephen Foster, who was the son of a Pennsylvania business man and who throughout his luckless thirty-eight years of life struggled vainly to make a living writing songs, wound up in a cheap New York boarding house and died at Bellevue Hospital, penniless and lonely. It seems a shame that his last moments could not have been brightened by the knowledge that within a very few decades his music would be honored by its inclusion under the heading of

Morton Gould

"American folksong." That such has been the happy fate of Foster's untutored but spontaneous art is no longer to be doubted, for of late years native composers have been irresistibly drawn to him and have made many arrangements of his songs, treating them as an authentic expression of the people. The latest of these arrangements, *Foster Gallery,* is the work of a talented young American, Morton Gould.

Purists may raise their eyebrows at the ingenious orchestral garb in which Gould has attired Foster; and they may well be right. Yet here is a thought to give them pause. When Glinka started working with Russian folksong material in an attempt to turn it into a polished and sophisticated native art, his efforts were regarded not as a sign of health but as tampering, and they elicited loud sneers. Yet it was just this tampering, or, rather, tapping of the native soil, that brought about a great flowering of Russian music.

A POSTSCRIPT

Distinct from all other contemporary developments, yet overshadowing them all, is the recent disintegration of Europe, shifting the center of gravity—in politics, in science, and in art—to the United States. This shift has had its repercussions in music. It has brought to this country leading European composers, fleeing from oppression at home; and it has centered attention on the heartening activity among native composers.

In the past, in spite of the fine accomplishments of such men as MacDowell and Griffes, American composers still clung to European models. Today they seem to have broken free, and it is felt that from now on this country will contribute its share of the world's masterpieces of music. Such names as Samuel Barber, Aaron Copland, Roy Harris, Charles Ives, Walter Piston, Quincy Porter, Roger Sessions, Virgil Thompson—are those of leading American "progressives." Many more names suggest themselves and if only a few of them have been mentioned in this book, the reason is that the orchestral works of most of these composers are as yet not available on discs.

Recommended Recordings

Compiled by

GEORGE C. LESLIE

THE GRAMOPHONE SHOP
18 EAST 48TH STREET, NEW YORK

Annotated by Paul Grabbe

NOTE: A more general list of recommended recordings is included in *The Story of One Hundred Symphonic Favorites,* a companion volume by the same author.

Symbols used in the following pages refer to record manufacturing companies, as follows:

AS - Anthologie Sonore (Gramoph. Shop)
C - Columbia
CM - Columbia Masterworks Set
D - Decca
FRM - Friends of Recorded Music
G - Gramophone (H.M.V.)
MC - Musicraft
PAR - Paraclete

Recommended Recordings

PD - Polydor
SC - Swarthmore College (Gramoph. Shop)
T - Telefunken
TI - Timely
V - Victor
VM - Victor Masterpiece Set

A VALUABLE SERVICE .

Periodically issued record supplements containing critical reviews of new releases (helpful when buying records) are obtainable for a relatively negligible subscription fee from:

The Gramophone Shop, 18 East 48th St., N. Y. C.—*H. Royer Smith Co.,* 10th and Walnut Streets, Philadelphia.

Very helpful, too, are the magazines *American Music Lover,* 45 Fourth Ave., N. Y. C., and *The Gramophone,* Montague House, Russell Square, London, England.

AN ALBUM NOT TO BE OVERLOOKED

Woodwind Family—Decca Little Symphony Orch. (Mendoza) 4–10″ in Set D–91.—This intelligently handled album contributes to the enjoyment of music by helping the listener learn to recognize the tone color of different instruments. And it is fun. In addition note companion sets: *Brass Family* (D–92); *String Family* (D–90); *Percussion Family* (D–93).

A GOOD BOOK TO HAVE

The Oxford Companion to Music by Percy A. Scholes. Oxford University Press, New York. —A one volume reference book on music and musicians which, in addition to being inexpensive—for what you get—and quite complete: a) brings out the human aspect of things, displaying a delightful sense of humor, a rare commodity in works of reference; b) is remarkably well cross-indexed and has many fascinating pictures.

A SET WELL OUT OF THE ORDINARY

Rhythm in the Jungle, Vol. I—Recorded by Laura C. Boulton on the Straus West African Expedition. 6–10″ with descriptive illustrated booklet, in Set V–P10.—When issued, this album of native African antiphonal singing and instrumental music created a sensation, for its rhythms (French Sudan, Nigeria, Timbuctu, British Cameroons) bring out the primitive in the most sophisticated.

Recommended Recordings

ALBENIZ, ISAAC (1860–1909)

Evocation and Triana (from Iberia) **G.** Novaes
(piano) 12″ No. C–71171D.—Two richly hued
pieces by the adventurous Andalusian, the
first modern Spaniard to exploit in serious
composition the treasures of his country's
musical folk idiom. See Liadov listing.

BACH, C. P. EMANUEL (1714–1788)

Concerto in D Major (arr. Steinberg)—Boston
Symph. (Koussevitzky) 2–12″ in Set VM–559.—
An interesting work by the remarkable 5th
child of Johann Sebastian, who, intended by
his father for the law, became a musician and
died in obscurity though a pioneer of highest
importance in the development of the sonata-
symphony form. Note particularly his *Mag-
nificat in D* (VM–444).

Recommended Recordings

BACH, J. CHRISTIAN (1735–1782)

Harpsichord Concerto in G Major—Roesgen-Champion & String Trio. 2–10″ Nos. v–4441/2.—A tuneful work by the 18th child of Johann Sebastian; musically a more relaxed member of the family, chiefly important because of his influence on Mozart and commonly referred to as the "English Bach" because of his long sojourn in London.

BACH, JOHANN SEBASTIAN (1685–1750)

Concerto (2 violins and orch.) in D Minor (1717–23)—J. Szigeti & C. Flesch with harpsichord and orch. (Goehr) 2–12″ in Set cm–x90. See page 30.

Nine Chorale-Preludes (1746?)—C. Weinrich (organ) 5–10″ in Set mc–22. The Bach here revealed is not the builder of towering musical structures, but the craftsman-miniaturist creating works of delicate but superb workmanship. Also note the quietly inspiring *Jesu, Joy of Man's Desiring* (Myra Hess, piano, v–4538); the masterly *"Dorian" Toccata and Fugue* for organ (Weinrich, in mc–37). In this connection see Buxtehude. Note in addition the complete *St. Matthew Passion* (vm–411, 412, 413) so overwhelming, it has been said no man can hear it through and fail to be left shaken and silent. (To sample this monu-

mental work note the final chorus, v–14661, a
noteworthy isolated record).

BALAKIREFF, MILI (1837–1910)

Thamar (1866–1882)—Paris Conserv. Orch.
(Coppola) 2–12″ Nos. v–11349/50. See page
68.

BARBER, SAMUEL (b. 1910)

Essay for Orchestra, Op. 12—Philadelphia Orch.
(Ormandy) 12″ No. v–18062. Impressive and
of excellent craftsmanship from the pen of a
promising young American.

BEETHOVEN, L. VAN (1770–1827)

Symphony No. 3 in E-flat Major—"Eroica"
(1804)—N. Y. Philharmonic (B. Walter) 6–12″
in Set cm–449. See page 50.—Of the many
available recordings of the other symphonies,
note the following first choices, most of them
truly inspired readings: Beecham's of No. 2
(cm–302); Furtwangler's of No. 5 (vm–426);
Toscanini's of No. 4 (vm–676) & No. 6
(vm–417); Weingartner's of No. 1 (cm–321) &
No. 7 (cm–260) & No. 9 (cm–227), which is the
best until Weingartner re-records); Mendel-
berg's of No. 8 (t–nsk2760/2)

Overture—Consecration of the House (1822)
—London Philharm. (Weingartner) 2–12″
in Set cm–x140.—Regarded as B's best over-

Recommended Recordings

ture. Note also the *String Quartet No. 14, Op. 131,* considered his greatest (vm–369); also, Gieseking's version of the *Piano Sonata No. 28, Op. 101,* one of the top-ranking works of B's maturity (cm–x172); also, Koussevitzky's fine reading of the difficult *Missa Solemnis* (vm–758 & 759).

BERG, ALBAN (1885–1935)

Concerto for Violin and Orchestra (1935)— L. Krasner & Cleveland Orch. (Rodzinski) 3–12″ in Set cm–456.—By the atonal disciple of Schönberg who has here produced something truly inspired—conceived as a Requiem in memory of a friend; completed four months before his own untimely death from infection.

BERLIOZ, HECTOR (1803–1869)

Fantastic Symphony (1829–30)—The Cleveland Orchestra (A. Rodzinski) 6–12″ in Set cm–488. See page 56.

The Trojans (1856–59) Overture—Paris Symphony Orch. (Monteux) 12″ No. v–11141.— Reveals the super-romantic B. as the possessor of a classical strain. Note from the same work the *Royal Hunt and Storm* (c–68043d); the *March* (d–25540); and the remarkable *Vain Regrets* from Act III (G. Thill & Chorus, c–9098m).

Recommended Recordings

BIZET, GEORGES (1838–1875)

Carmen (1875) Suite—London Philharmonic (Beecham) 2–12″ in Set CM–X144. Or, complete opera by Paris Opéra-Comique; 15–12″ in Set CM–01. See page 76.

Petite Suite (1873)—London Philharmonic (Dorati) 2–12″ in Set VM–510.—A charming work which helped the hard-pressed Bizet, won him wider recognition, and was later absorbed into the ballet repertoire as "Jeux d'Enfants." Note also the suites from *l'Arlesienne:* No. 1 (Stokowski, VM–62); No. 2 (Fiedler, VM–683)—music which has weathered the years and remains as fresh and vital as ever.

BLISS, ARTHUR (b. 1891)

Music for Strings (1936)—B. B. C. Symphony (Boult) 3–12″ in Set VM–464. See p. 162.

Quintet for clarinet and strings (1932)—
F. Thurston & Griller Quartet. 4–12" Nos.
D–K780/3. ". . . a work worthy to stand be-
side Mozart and Brahms in a program, although utterly unlike either . . . but repre-
sentative of modern chamber music at its
best." (Eric Blom)

BLOCH, ERNEST (b. 1880)

Schelomo (1915–16)—E. Feuermann (cello) and
Philadelphia Orch. (Stokowski) 3–12" in Set
VM–698. See page 138. Also note B's *Concerto
Grosso for Piano and String Orchestra* (VM–
563) and his interesting *Piano Quintet* (VM–
191).

BORODIN, ALEXANDER (1833–1887)

Prince Igor (begun 1869) Excerpts—Leeds Fest.
Choir & London Philharm. (Beecham) 2–12"
in Set CM–X54. See page 72. From the same
work note *Arioso of Jaroslavna* (Nina Koshetz,
V–9233) and *No sleep, no rest* (Baklanov,
D–25122). Note also the little masterpiece *In
the Steppes of Central Asia* (Coates, V–11169)
which depicts a caravan crossing the desert.

BRAHMS, JOHANNES (1833–1897)

Symphony No. 2, in D Major (1877)—London
Philharmonic (Weingartner) 5–12", Set CM–493.
See page 78. Regarding the other symphonies

note Weingartner's version of No. 1 (CM–383)
& No. 3 (CM–353); Koussevitzky's version of
No. 4 (VM–730).

Variations on a Theme by Haydn (1873)—
Luboshutz & Nemenoff (duo pianists) 2–12″ in
Set VM–799—or, London Philharmonic (Weingartner) 2–12″ in Set CM–X125.—A choice between these is a matter of personal preference;
one displays B. working in a medium he particularly enjoyed; the other marks his first mature orchestral effort. Note also the *Quintet
(Clarinet & Strings) Op. 115*, notable as one of
the most heart-warming pieces written (Kell &
Busch Quartet, VM–491); the set of *Five Inter-
mezzi*—aptly nicknamed "mighty miniatures"
—for piano (Gieseking, CM–201); the fine album (L. Lehman, in German) of B's songs
(CM–453).

BRUCKNER, ANTON (1824–1896)

Symphony No. 9 in D Minor (1894) Original
Edition—Munich Philharm. (von Hausegger)
7–12″ in Set VM–627. See page 98. Also note
the long neglected *Symphony No. 5 in B-flat
Major* (1876) nicknamed "Tragic" in Set VM–
770.

BUXTEHUDE, DIETRICH (1637–1707)

Organ Music. Carl Weinrich. 4–12″ in Set
MC–40.—A superb collection of works by Bux-

tehude from whose art twenty-year-old Johann
Sebastian Bach (who trudged 200 miles on foot
to hear the aging master) learned a lot.

CHABRIER, ALEXIS (1841–1894)

Rhapsody Espana (1883)—London Phil. Orchestra (Beecham) 12"C–71250D. See page 88.—
Many composers have written works Spanish
in feeling. This suggests an interesting comparison: what Spain meant to another Frenchman—see Debussy's Iberia; to a Russian—
Rimsky's Capriccio; a Hungarian cosmopolite
—Liszt's Rhapsody; a Spaniard—de Falla's
Nights.

Cotillon-Ballet—London Philharm. (Dorati)
2–12" in Set CM–X113.—A delightful musical
divertissement, originally for the piano, now a
Ballet-Russe item. Note also his ebullient
Bourrée Fantasque (Meyrowitz, No. C–17108D).

CHAUSSON, ERNEST (1855–1899)

Poem for Violin and Orchestra (1896)—Yehudi
Menuhin & Paris Symph. (Enesco) 2–12"
Nos. V–7913/4. See page 100. Note also his
Symphony in B-flat Major (VM–261).

CHAVEZ, CARLOS (b. 1899)

Music of Chavez—includes Sinfonia de Antigona
(1933) and *Sinfonia India* (1936); also a Bux-

tehude Chaconne, orchestrated by Chavez. Symphony Orch. of Mexico (Chavez) 4–12" in Set VM–503. See page 156.

CHOPIN, FRÉDÉRIC (1810–1849)

Les Sylphides Ballet—Excerpts arr. Douglas. London Philharm. (Goehr) 12" No. C–69281D. —Although Chopin's medium was the piano (he produced only two orchestral works of note, 2 piano concertos, VM–418 & 567) few will quarrel with the above sparkling arrangements. Those preferring Chopin "straight" will find him in the *Mazurkas* (Arth. Rubinstein, VM–626, 656 & 691); the *Preludes* (Cortot, VM–282); the *Ballades* (Cortot, VM–399).

COPLAND, AARON (b. 1900)

El Salón México (1936)—Boston Sym. (Koussevitzky) 2–12" in Set VM–546.—Taking its name from a ballroom in Mexico City, one of the tourists' "hot spots," this picturesque, if somewhat brittle tonal picture displays C's fine satirical sense and excellent craftsmanship.

CORELLI, ARCANGELO (1653–1713)

Concerto Grosso in G-Minor (Christmas Concerto) Op. 6, No. 8 (1712)—London Symphony Orch. (Walter) 2–12" in Set VM–600. See page 26. Also note the charming *Concerto Grosso in B-flat Major, Op. 6, No. 11* (Fiedler's Simfonietta, V–13587).

Recommended Recordings

COUPERIN, FRANCOIS (1668–1733)

Lecon de Ténèbres No. 3 (1713–15) arr. Hoerée.
Derenne, Cuénod (tenors), Archimbaud
(treble), Wetchor (soprano), Adriano (trumpet)
de Lacour (harpsichord), Braquemond (organ)
with chorus and orchestra (Evrard) 2–12″
Nos. v–12325/6. See page 28. Also note C's
Concert Royal No. 2. 12″ No. as–13.

DEBUSSY, CLAUDE (1862–1918)

La Mer (1903–05)—Boston Symph. (Koussevitzky) 3–12″ in Set vm–643. See p. 116.

Pagodes (Estampes No. 1) & *L'Isle Joyeuse*—
Gieseking (piano) 12″ No. c–69841d—Two of
D's most interesting piano pieces. Also note
his famous *Afternoon of a Faun* (Beecham—c–
69600d) and see Chabrier with regard to his
Iberia (cm–491). In addition note D's orchestral *Nocturnes; Clouds; Festivals; Sirens* (Phila.
Orch., Stokowski, vm–630).

Recommended Recordings

DELIUS, FREDERICK (1862–1934)

Delius Society, Vol. III—London Philharm., B. B. C. chorus (Beecham) 7–12″ in Set CM–355. See page 114.

In addition to *Appalachia* (1902), album contains the closing scene from *Hassan* (1920); a dance from *Koanga* (1897); a prelude (1931) to the opera *Irmelin*.

On Hearing the First Cuckoo in Spring (1912) —London Philharm. (Lambert). 10″ No. v–4496.—One of D's finest short works, projecting "in unforgettable tones the emotions of spring." (Heseltine)

DOHNÁNYI, ERNO (b. 1877)

Symphonic Minutes (1935)—Queen's Hall Or. (Wood) 2–12″ in Set D–6. See p. 160.—For pleasant listening note also the orchestral *Suite in F-sharp Minor* (VM–47); by no means as succinct as the Minutes but in the characteristic D. vein.

DVOŘÁK, ANTONIN (1841–1904)

Slavonic Dances, Op. 46 (1878)—Czech Philharm. (Talich) 4–10″ in Set VM–310. See page 80 & Liadov listing.

Symphony No. 2 in D Minor, Op. 70 (1885)— Czech Philharm. (Talich) 5–12″ in Set vm–663. Among D's best; ranked by authorities alongside of Brahms' symphonies. (For the 2nd set of Slav. Dances, 1886, note vm–345; for the ever popular symphony *From the New World*, 1893, see vm–469).

ELGAR, SIR EDWARD (1857–1934)

Enigma Variations, Op. 36 (1899)—Queen's Hall Orch. (Wood) 4–12″ Nos. D–25739/42. See page 104. Note also his *Introduction and Allegro for Strings* (vm–635) as well as No. 1 & No. 4 of the set of *Pomp and Circumstance Marches* with which E's name has become so closely linked (c–70364D).

FALLA, MANUEL DE (b. 1876)

Nights in the Gardens of Spain (1909–15)—L. Descaves (piano) with Paris Conserv. Orch. (Bigot) 3–12″ in Set vm–725. See page 136.

Three-Cornered Hat, Ballet Suite (1919)—Boston "Pops" Orch. (Fiedler) 2–10″ in Set vm–505.—Delightful music, but those seeking the quintessence of de Falla and Spain should not miss acquaintance with the *Seven Popular Spanish Songs* (1914) as sung by Conchita Supervia. 3–10″ Nos. D–20288/90. See Liadov.

FAURÉ, GABRIEL (1845–1924)

Requiem, Op. 48 (1887)—S. Dupont (soprano), M. Didier (bass), E. Commette (organ) with

Recommended Recordings

chorus & orch. (Bourmauck) 5–12″ in Set
CM–354. See page 92. As an interesting com-
parison with the serenely devotional spirit of
Fauré (a Roman Catholic) note the more
effulgent expressions of faith by Tchaikovsky,
Archangelsky, etc. (Greek Orthodox or
Eastern Church) in *Russian Liturgical Music*,
VM–768. Compare both with the great (Prot-
estant) religious works of J. S. Bach.

Elegie, Op. 24 (1883)—J. Benedetti (cello) &
Boston Symph. (Koussevitzky) 12″ No. V–14577.
—A work of mellowed, penetrating warmth.
Also note the famous *Piano Quartet* (VM–594);
the collection of songs, interpreted by Panzéra
(VM–478), an album greatly prized as the best
France has to offer in this field.

FRANCK, CÉSAR (1822–1890)

Symphonic Variations (1885)—Alfred Cortot
(piano) and London Philharm. (Wood) 2–12″
Nos. V–8357/8. See page 90.

Les Éolides, Symphonic Poem (1876); includes
pieces by Couperin. C. B. Symphony (Barlow)
2–12″ in Set CM–X145.—An early but charming piece. Also note 3 outstanding mature
works: the justly famous *Chorale, Prelude and
Fugue* for the piano (E. Petri, CM–X176); the
broodingly exalted *D Minor Symphony* (San
Francisco Symph., P. Monteux, VM–840); and

[186]

Recommended Recordings

the great organ *Chorale No. 3 in A Minor*
(included in Courboin's VM–695).

FRESCOBALDI, G. (1583–1643)

Toccata for the Elevation—Marcel Dupré (organ) 12" No. AS–4.—By the famous 17th
century musician whose appointment as organist to St. Peter's in Rome is said to have
drawn a crowd of 30,000 to hear his first performance. Note particularly F's *Toccata*
(V–17632) in Hans Kindler's sympathetic tran-
scription for orchestra.

GERSHWIN, GEORGE (1898–1937)

A Gershwin Album—Paul Whiteman Orch. &
Bargy & Linda, pianists. 5–12" in Set D–31.
—One of the most interesting journeys of
exploration into the more serious aspects of
G's music. Contains the *Rhapsody in Blue*
(compare page 144; the little known *Second
Rhapsody; An American in Paris;* and the
really thrilling *Cuban Overture.*

GLINKA, MICHAEL I. (1803–1857)

Kamarinskaya (1848)—London Symph. Orch.
(Coates) 12" No. V–11482. See page 62. Note
also, for comparison, ballet music from
Roussalka (C–69126D) by Dargomijsky, G's
co-worker successor in the creation of national
Russian music.

Recommended Recordings

GLUCK, CHRISTOPH W. (1714–1787)

Iphigénie En Aulide (1774)—Overture. Includes Corelli's Adagio. C. B. Symphony (Barlow) 2–12″ in Set CM–X138. See p. 36. Also note *Ballet-Suite No. 1* (VM–787) which contains other music from Iphigénie, in addition to excerpts from Armide, Don Juan, and from Orfeo ed Euridice, earliest opera still regularly produced.

GOULD, MORTON (b. 1913)

Foster Gallery (1939)—Boston "Pops" Orch. (Fiedler) 2–12″ in Set VM–727. See page 168. —Those preferring a straight orchestral version will note that of Kostelanetz, CM–442; those still not satisfied will find Frank Luther's unaffected singing (accompanied by violin, piano, guitar, banjo, in D–1996/2000) a faithful reflection of Foster's own age.

Recommended Recordings

GRANADOS, ENRIQUE (1867–1916)

12 Spanish Dances—G. Cazes (piano) 6–10″ Nos.
D–20653/8.   Youthful and vibrant, by the
talented Spaniard whose life was cut short
by a German torpedo. See Liadov.

GRIEG, EDVARD (1843–1907)

Norwegian Dances, Op. 35 (1881) Nos. 1 & 4.
—Grand Orch. Symphonique (Ruhlmann)
12″ No. c–P69409D.   The complete set of
four dances is obtainable in an older recording
v–11456/7. See p. 86 & Liadov.

Symphonic Dances, Op. 64 (1885–90)—Berlin
Philharm. (Dobrowen) 2–12″ Nos. D–25241/2.
—Romantic and rugged, these pieces approxi-
mate the perfection of the Norwegian Dances,
Op. 35. For two of G's loveliest songs, note
v–15180.

HANDEL, GEORGE F. (1685–1759)

Alcina (1735) Suite—Paris Conservatory Orchestra (Weingartner) 2–12″ in Set cM–x164. See
page 32.

Concerto No. 1 (Oboe & Orch.) in B-flat Maj.
—Leon Goossens and London Philharm.
(Eugene Goossens) 12″ No. v–12605.—A late
work, published posthumously, it is also one
of H's happiest; delightfully jaunty, un-

Recommended Recordings

flaggingly melodious. Also note the *Faithful Shepherd Suite,* arr. Beecham (CM-458).

HANSON, HOWARD (b. 1896)

Symphony No. 2—"Romantic" (1930)—Rochester Symph. (Hanson) 4-12″ in Set VM-648. See page 152. Note also the ingratiating *Merry Mount Suite* (VM-781).

HARRIS, ROY (b. 1898)

Symphony No. 3 (1938)—Boston Symph. (Koussevitzky) 2-12″ in Set VM-651. See p. 166.

Chorale from String Sextet (1932)—Kreiner Sextet. 12″ No. V-12537.—The theme of this work is "taken from the melodic contours of early American church tunes." (Harris)

HAYDN, JOSEPH (1732–1809)

Symphony No. 102 in B-flat Major, Salomon Series No. 9 (1794)—Boston Symph. (Koussevitzky) 3-12″ in Set VM-529. See p. 40.

Concerto for Trumpet and Orchestra (Andante & Rondo, only)—G. Eskdale & Symph. Orch. (Goehr) 12″ No. C-70106D.—Unusually enjoyable though little known. Also note the marvelous blend of court and countryside in *Symphony No. 93 in D Major,* (Beecham, CM-336) first of the 12 symphonies composed in 1791 for the impressario Salomon.

[190]

Recommended Recordings

HINDEMITH, PAUL (b. 1895)

Symphony—Mathis the Painter (1934) Berlin Philharm. (Hindemith) 3–12″ Nos. T–E1647/9 or, Philadelphia Orchestra (Ormandy) 3–12″ in Set VM–854. See page 158.

String Quartet No. 3 Op. 22 (1922)—The Coolidge Quartet. 3–12″ in Set VM–524.—A nervously high-spirited work which dates from the period when Germany lay prostrate. "Here we find negation, scorn, and the forced merriment with which those affected sought to stifle despair." (Edwin Evans). Almost, if not quite as interesting is H's *Sonata for Viola and Piano, Op. 11 No. 4* (VM–547) which dates from the same unhappy year, 1922.

HOLST, GUSTAV (1874–1934)

St. Paul's Suite—Boyd Neel Orch. 2–10″ Nos. D–20171/2.—Unpretentious and gay, surely of finer vintage than the more highly publicized, over-grandiose *The Planets* (CM–359) by this Britisher. Do not overlook H's splendid song *Mid-Winter* (Madrigal Singers, unacc. No. C–321M).

HONNEGER, ARTHUR (b. 1892)

King David (1921)—Soloists, chorus, and orchestra. 3–12″ Nos. C–68937D and D–25517/8.—Some interesting excerpts from the dramatic

psalm by the modern Frenchman of Swiss
descent more generally known by his symphonic vision of a locomotive, *Pacific 231*
(D–25206).

IBERT, JAQUES (b. 1890)

Ports of Call (Escales) Suite (1922)—Esraram
Orch. 2–12″ CM–X16. See page 142.

The Little White Donkey—E. Boynet (piano)
10″ No. V–4315.—A delectable item exhibiting
I's fine sense of humor. Also note his
Divertissement, VM–324.

INDY, VINCENT D' (1851–1931)

*Symphony on a French Mountain Air for Piano
and Orchestra* (1886)—J. Darré and Lamou-
reux Orch, (Wolff) 3–12″ Nos. D–CA8123/5.
—Probably unobtainable until end of war
but listed here as representing the best of
this eminent French composer, educator, lover
of nature, and pupil of César Franck.

KODÁLY, ZOLTÁN (b. 1882)

Háry János—Suite (1925-26)—Minneapolis Symphony (Ormandy) 3–12″ in Set VM–197. See
page 146. For a more serious side of Kodály,
note his eloquent song *Evening* (Augustana
Choir, unacc. No. V–1937). Also note the interesting *Dances from Galanta.* (Fiedler, VM–
834) composed in 1934.

Recommended Recordings

LIADOV, ANATOL (1855–1914)

Russian Folksongs (1906)—Philadelphia Orch. (Stokowski) 12″ & 10″ Nos. V–8491/1681. See page 118. Also, for an interesting comparison of folk-song material in the hands of composers of note, see recordings of Vaughan Williams, Dvorak, Grieg, Falla, Granados, Albeniz, Gould.

LISZT, FRANZ (1811–1886)

Faust Symphony (1854–57)—Paris Philharm. with M. Villabella (tenor) and Vlassov Choir (Meyrowitz) 7–12″ in Set CM–272. See page 64.

Spanish Rhapsody (1845) arr. for piano & orch. by Busoni. E. Petri and Minneapolis Symph. (Mitropoulos) 2–12″ in Set CM–X163. See Chabrier listing. Also, when war's end makes records available, note especially any of the *Hungarian Rhapsodies* as played by

Recommended Recordings

pianist A. Borowsky (PD–561113/8 & 566181/7)
—pieces reputedly bombastic but undeservedly
maligned.

LULLY, JEAN BAPTISTE (1632–1687)

Orchestral Excerpts from four operas: *Thé-
sée* (1675); *Atys* (1676); *Proserpine* (1680);
Amadis (1684)—Orch. Symph. (Cauchie) 2–10″
in Set CM–376. See page 14. Also note *Opera
Airs,* in French with String Orch. (AS–20.)

MACDOWELL, EDWARD (1861–1908)

"Indian" Suite (1897)—C. M. Symphony (Barlow)
4–12″ in Set CM–373. See page 102. Also note
M's zestful *Piano Concerto No. 2* (Sanroma;
Fiedler; VM–324).

MAHLER, GUSTAV (1860–1911)

The Song of the Earth (1908–09)—C. Kullman,
tenor; K. Thorborg, contralto, with Vienna
Philharm. (Walter) 7–12″ in Set CM–300. See
page 124. For two of M's most engaging
lighter songs note C–17241D.

MENDELSSOHN, FELIX (1809–1847)

Concerto (Violin & Orchestra) in E Minor (1844)
—J. Szigeti & Royal Philharmonic (Beecham)
4–12″ in Set CM–190. See p. 60.

Symphony No. 5 in D Major—"*Reformation*"
(1830–32)—C. B. Symphony (Barlow) 4–12″ in

Recommended Recordings

Set CM–391.—Contains some grand moments, but to many the cream of M's inspiration is contained in the sparkling *'Italian' Symphony* (Koussevitzky, VM–294); the delicately effervescent *Overture from 'A Midsummer Night's Dream'* (Fiedler, V–11919/20); the intensely glowing *Hebrides—'Fingal's Cave'—Overture* (Beecham, C–6940OD).

MILHAUD, DARIUS (b. 1892)

Creation of the World (1923)—Symph. Orchestra (Milhaud) 2–12″ in Set CM–X18. See page 144 & Gershwin recordings. Also note the briskly good-humored and spicy *Scaramouche Suite* for 2 pianos (Bartlett and Robertson—C–69835D).

MONTEVERDI, CLAUDIO (1567–1643)

Orfeo (1607)—Soloists & chorus with organ, harpsichord & orchestra (Calusio) 12–12″ obtainable through Gramophone Shop N. Y. but not until after war. Meantime note M's arias and madrigals sung by soprano and contralto from Opera Comique accompanied by instrumental ensemble (Crussard) 12″ No. V–15466; and *Ohimé, ch'io cado* (AS–21). See p. 10.

MOUSSORGSKY, MODESTE (1839–1881)

Boris Godounov (1868; rev. 1872) Symphonic

Synthesis, arr. Stokowski from original (not Rimsky-Korsakov's) score.—Philadelphia Orch. (Stokowski) 3–12″ in Set VM–391. See page 70. From the same work note Chaliapin records, V–11485, V–14517, V–15177. In addition note *Prelude to Khovantchina* (Koussevitzky, V–14415); the brilliantly etched *Pictures at an Exhibition* (Koussevitzky, VM–102).

MOZART, WOLFGANG A. (1756–1791)

Symphony No. 34 in C Major, K–338 (1780) London Philharm. (Beecham) 3–12″ in Set CM–123. See page 38. (Beecham's new recording, issued in England, has not yet been released here by Columbia).

Serenade No. 10 in B-flat Major for thirteen wind instruments, K–361 (1780)—Chamber Orchestra (Fischer) 3–12″ in Set VM–743.— Intense and searching in spite of the odd combination of instruments. Also note *Symphony No. 39 in E-flat Major,* K–543, the 1st of M's three greatest (Beecham, CM–456).

OFFENBACH, JAQUES (1819–1890)

Selections of Can-Cans—Light Symphony Orch. 12″ No. V–36213.—A testimonial to the exuberance of this XIXth century genius of musical burlesque. Reverse side contains selections of Polkas from two other masters of light music, Johan and Joseph Strauss.

Recommended Recordings

PISTON, WALTER (b. 1894)

Suite from "The Incredible Flutist" (1938)—
Boston "Pops" Orch. (Fiedler) 2–12″ in Set
VM–621.—Selections from the amusing ballet
by a gifted American.

PROKOFIEFF, SERGE (b. 1891)

Classical Symphony (1917)—Boston Symph.
(Koussevitzky) 2–12″ Nos. V–7196/7. See page
140.

Concerto (Violin & Orchestra) No. 2 in G Minor
(1935)—J. Heifetz & Boston Symphony (Koussevitzky) 3–12″ in Set VM–450.—Lyrical, almost epic, in sharp contrast to P's former
tartly sophisticated frolics, as in the Classical
Symphony, or the "diabolical brutality," as
the critics cried out, of his *Violin Concerto
No. 1* (Szigeti & Beecham, CM–244) or even
his *Piano Concerto No. 3* (VM–176). Note
also the satyrical *Lieutenant Kije* (VM–459);
the *String Quartet* (CM–448).

PURCELL, HENRY (1659–1695)

New Suite (arr, Barbirolli) containing excerpts
from P's inimitable "Dramatick Musick":
Dido and Aeneas (1689); *King Arthur* (1691);
The Gordian Knot (1691) and *The Virtuous
Wife* (1694)—N. Y. Philharm. Symph. Orch.
(Barbirolli) 2–12″ in Set VM–533. See p. 16. Also,

Recommended Recordings

The English Music Society, Vol. I—Contains the
most rounded sampling of P's music: some
rollicking catches and airs; several instrumental fantasias, unequaled (some 50 years
later) by Sebastian Bach himself; also includes
the famous *Golden Sonata*. (3–10″ & 5–12″ in
Set CM–315).

RACHMANINOFF, SERGEI (b. 1873)

The Isle of the Dead, Tone Poem (1907)—
Philadelphia Orch. (Rachmaninoff); album
includes R's *Vocalise*, Op. 34. 3–12″ in Set
VM–75. See page 120.

Rhapsody on a Theme by Paganini, Op. 43.
(1934)—Rachmaninoff (piano) with Philadelphia Orch. (Stokowski) 3–12″ in Set VM–
250—" . . . carries us back immediately to
the Rachmaninoff of the richest creative
period . . ." (Kolodin). Also note his two
most famous works: *Piano Concerto No. 2*
(Rachmaninoff; Stokowski; VM–58) and *Symphony No. 2* (Ormandy, VM–239).

RAMEAU, JEAN P. (1683–1764)

Three Ballet Pieces for Orchestra (arr. Mottl)
Includes excerpts from Les Fetes d'Hebé
(1739) and Platée (1749)—Boston "Pops" Orch.
(Fiedler) 2–10″ No. V–4431/2. See page 34.
Also note R's *Fifth Piece for Clavecin* (AS–30).

Recommended Recordings

RAVEL, MAURICE (1875–1937)

Pavane for a dead Infanta (1899 & 1912)—Concert Colonne (Pierné) 12" No. D-25416. See page 130.

Introduction and Allegro for Harp with accompaniment by String Quartet, Flute, and Clarinet (1906)—Laura Newell, Stuyvesant String Quartet, Wummer & McLane. 2–12" in Set CM-X167.—A hauntingly beautiful work. Also note the intriguing *Gaspard de la Nuit* (Gieseking, piano, CM-X141); and the second suite from R's masterpiece *Daphnis and Chloé* (Boston Symph. Koussevitzky, V-7143/4).

RESPIGHI, OTTORINO (1879–1936)

The Birds (Gli Ucelli) Suite (1927)—Brussels Conserv. Orch. (Defauw) 2–12" in Set CM-X108. See page 148.

Impressioni Brasiliane (1927)—Munich Philharm. (Kabasta) 2–12" Nos. G-DB4643/4.—Written during a visit to Brazil, these impressions are among R's best. Records may be unavailable until end of war unless Victor issues domestically. Also note *Rustic Dance* (Barbirolli, V-17558).

RIMSKY-KORSAKOFF, N. (1884–1908)

Scheherazade—Symphonic Suite (1888)—Cleveland Orch. (Rodzinski) 5–12″ in Set CM–398. See page 94.

Spanish Capriccio, Op. 34 (1887)—Boston "Pops" Orch. (Fiedler) 2–12″ Nos. V–11827/8.—Always scrupulously honest (and modest) R-K called the Capriccio merely "a showpiece." Be this as it may, the work is unsurpassed as an example of 19th century orchestral wizardry. See Chabrier listing.

ROSSINI, GIOACCHINO (1792–1868)

La Boutique Fantastique—London Philharm. (Goossens) 3–12″ in Set VM–415.—An arrangement for the ballet by Respighi of some of Rossini's best tunes. These enchanted music lovers 100 years ago but retain enough vitality to delight even today.

SAINT-SAËNS, CAMILLE (1835–1921)

Concerto (Cello & Orch.) No. 1 in A Minor

(1873)—G. Piatigorsky & Chicago Symph.
(Stock) 2–12″ in Set CM–X182. See p. 74.
Note also the intriguing *Scherzo for two Pianos*
(C–70740D); the *Bacchanale from Act III of
Samson and Delila* (Fiedler, V–12318); the
popular *Danse Macabre* (Stock, C–11251D);
the great *Third Symphony* (Coppola, VM–100).

SCARLATTI, DOMENICO (1685–1757)

The Good Humored Ladies—Ballet Suite—
London Philharm. (Goossens) 2–12″ in Set
VM–512.—From the pen of the famed 18th
century harpsichord virtuoso, these captivat-
ing keyboard pieces gain rather than lose
in Tommasini's deft arrangement for orchestra. Also note the brilliantly played *Sonatas*
(Cassadesus, piano, CM–372). For a sampling
of the music of Domenico's father, Alessandro
Scarlatti (1659–1725), preeminent as a pioneer
in opera, note the *Sonata a Quattro* (Stuyvesant
Quartet, C–17214D).

SCHÖNBERG, ARNOLD (b. 1874)

Gurre-Lieder (1900–1911)—Philadelphia Orch.
(Stokowski) 14–12″ in Set VM–127. See page
126.

Verklärte Nacht, Op. 4 (1899)—Minneapolis
Symph. (Ormandy) 4–12″ in Set VM–207.—A
work "completely at home in the world of

[201]

romantic harmony." (P. Stefan). But note
the subsequent *Pierrot Lunaire* (CM–461?
characterized by critics 30 years ago as "the
most ear-splitting combination of tones that
ever desecrated the walls of a Berlin music
hall;"—today, not quite so "ear-splitting" but
still one of the controversial works of the
century.

SCHUBERT, FRANZ (1797–1828)

Symphony No. 9 in C Major (1828)—Chicago
Symph. Orch. (Stock) 6–12″ in Set CM–403.
See page 54.

Five German Dances (1813)—N. Y. Philharm.
(Barbirolli) 2–10″ Nos. V–2162/3.—So charming, it is hard to believe that they sprang from
S's bleak and hungry adolescence. Note also
the "Unfinished" *Symphony No. 8* (Beecham,
CM–330); the complete *Rosamunde music*
(Harty, CM–343); the great *String Quartet, Op.*
163 (Pro Arte, VM–299); the songs (E. Schumann, VM–497).

SCHUMANN, ROBERT (1810–1856)

Symphony No. 1 in B-flat Major—"Spring"
(1841)—Boston Symph. (Koussevitzky) 4–12″ in
Set VM–655. See page 58.

Three Romances for Oboe and Piano (1849)—
L. Goossens & G. Moore. 2–12″ in Set

CM–X160.—". . . the most attractive things he ever wrote." (J. A. Fuller-Maitland). Note also *Carnaval* (Myra Hess, piano, VM–476) and the same work in Glazounov's orch. arrangement for the ballet (Eugene Goossens, VM–513); the *Piano Concerto in A Minor* (Myra Hess; Goehr; VM–473); the invigorating *Piano Quintet, Op. 44* (A. Schnabel: Pro Arte Quartet; VM–267).

SCHÜTZ, HEINRICH (1585–1672)

3 Geistliche Concerte (1636–39) — Max Meili (tenor), Suter-Moser (soprano), le Marc Hadour (baritone), Cellier (organ) 12″ No. AS–28. See p. 12. Also note his impressive *Passion Music* (1665–66) as sung by soloists & Swarthmore College Choir. 4–12″ in Set SC–2, obt. through Gramoph. Shop.

SCRIABIN, ALEXANDER (1872–1915)

Poem of Ecstasy (1907–08) with *Prometheus* (1909–10)—Philadelphia Orch. (Stokowski) 4–12″ in Set VM–125. See p. 122. For examples of S's piano music note *Selected Piano Pieces,* played by Samuel Yaffe (2–10″ PAR–6/7; and 7–10″ Nos. PAR 8, 9, 12, 15/18).

SHOSTAKOVICH, DMITRI (b. 1906)

Symphony No. 5, Op. 47 (1937)—Philadelphia

Recommended Recordings

Orch. (Stokowski) 6–12″ in Set VM–619. See page 164.

Two Pieces for String Octet—Octet of the N. Y. Simfonietta (Goberman) 12″ No. TI–1300.—A dreamy prelude and a spirited scherzo, with just enough dissonance to make them spicy. Also note S's *Symphony No. 1* (CM–472), now in vogue also as a ballet called "Rouge et Noire," and *Symphony No. 6* (Stokowski, VM–867).

SIBELIUS, JEAN (b. 1865)

Sibelius Society, Vol. VI—London Philharm. (Beecham) 7–12″ in Set VM–658. Covers 34 years, with some of S's best represented. Contains, in addition to *The Bard* (1913), the early, delightful *En Saga* (1892), the suite *Pélleas and Mélisande* (1905), the funeral march *In Memoriam* (1909) and the *Prelude to The Tempest* (1926). See page 132.

Rakastava (The Lover) Suite, Op. 14 (1893)—Boyd Neel Orch. 2–12″ Nos. D–25730/1.—Not widely known but first-ranking among S's minor works. Also, as the perfect introduction to S's music, note the haunting *Swan of Tuonela*. 12″ No. C–11388D. Also note symphonies: No. 1 (Kajanus. CM–151); No. 4 (Beecham, VM–446); Nos. 2 & 5 (Koussevitzky, VM–272 & VM–474).

Recommended Recordings

SMETANA, BEDRICH (1824–1884)

The Moldau—2nd from the cycle of six symphonic poems "My Country" (1874–79). Album also includes *From Bohemia's Meadows and Forests,* which is No. 4 from the same cycle. Others still unrecorded.—Czech Philharmonic (Kubelik) 3–12″ in Set VM–523. See page 82.

The Bartered Bride (1866) Excerpts—C. B. Symphony (Barlow) 12″ No. C–71049D.—Three boisterous dances from the famous opera which was taken up by S's countrymen as a rallying cry of Czech national life.

STILL, WILLIAM GRANT (b. 1895)

Scherzo from Afro-American Symphony (1931) Eastman Rochester Symph. (Hanson) 10″ No. V–2059.—A sample to whet the appetite from a major work of a talented American, "by far the most widely recognized Negro composer today." (J. T. Howard)

STRAUSS, JOHANN, 2nd (1825–1899)

Album of Strauss Waltzes—contains Wine, Women and Song; Wiener Blut; Artist's Life; Emperor and Frühlingstimmen.—Boston "Pops" Orch. (Fiedler) 1–10″ & 4–12″ in Set VM–445. Note the "Waltz King's" most famous piece, *On the Beautiful Blue Danube* (Stokow-

Recommended Recordings

ski, v–15425); also *Rediscovered Music* (Barlow, CM–389); and see *Polkas* under Offenbach.

STRAUSS, RICHARD (b. 1864)

Death and Transfiguration (1889)—Philadelphia Orch. (Stokowski) 3–12″ in Set VM–217. See page 96. Note also the symphonic poems *Don Juan* (Busch, VM–351) and *Also sprach Zarathustra* (Koussevitzky, VM–257) as well as the *Waltzes from Der Rosenkavalier* (Rodzinski, C–11542D).

STRAVINSKY, IGOR (b. 1882)

Petrouchka—Suite (1911)—Philadelphia Orch. (Stokowski) 4–12″ in Set VM–574. See page 128.

Symphony of Psalms (1930)—Vlassov Chorus & symph. orchestra (Stravinsky) 3–12″ in Set CM–162.—Revealing the religious aspect of the one time "horrible modernist" whose scenes of pagan Russia, *Rite of Spring* (CM–417) created such a stir when first produced in 1913. Also note *The Wedding* (CM–204) scored (!) for voices, 4 pianos, and 17 percussion instruments.

SULLIVAN, SIR ARTHUR (1842–1900)

H. M. S. Pinafore—complete by D'Oyly Carte Company. 9–12″ in Set v–C13.—Some of the other Gilbert & Sullivan works recorded by the same company are: *Trial by Jury* (v–c4); *Iolanthe* (v–c10); *The Mikado* (v–c26); *Pirates of Penzance* (v–c6); *The Gondoliers* (v–c16). Note in addition a good abridged version of *Iolanthe* (Columbia Light Opera Co., cm–422) and a fine medley arr. for orchestra from *Yeomen of the Guard* (d–25712).

TAYLOR, DEEMS (b. 1885)

Through the Looking Glass—Suite (1922)— C. B. Symphony (Barlow) 4–12″ in Set cm–350. —A musical version of Alice's adventures by the man who has done so much to make music more intelligible and more enjoyable to thousands of Americans.

TCHAIKOVSKY, PETER I. (1840–1893)

Serenade in C Major (1880)—B. B. C. Symphony (Boult) 3–12″ in Set vm–556. See p. 84. Also,

Recommended Recordings

Symphony No. 3 in D Major, Op. 29 (1875) Natl. Symph. Orch. (Kindler) 5–12″ in Set vm–747.—The Cinderella among T's symphonies; lovely but so far outbid by the more glamorous, noisier 4th & 5th; the gloomier 6th. (Best recording of the latter is Furtwangler's vm–553; of the 4th., Koussevitzky's vm–327; of the 5th., Rodzinski's exciting cm–406 or Beecham's subtle cm–470). Note also the *Waltz from Eugene Onegin* (v–4565) to the strains of which a whole generation grew up in Russia.

TURINA, JOAQUIN (b. 1882)

Rhapsodia Sinfonica—E. Joyce (piano) & Orch. (Raybould) 12″ No. d–25452.—Lyrical and much more directly appealing than the colorful but noisy "Procesion del Rocio" through which this Spanish composer has become so widely known.

VAUGHAN WILLIAMS, RALPH (b. 1872)

A London Symphony (1914)—Queen's Hall Orch. (Wood) 5–12″ Nos. d–25618/22. See p. 134. (The Pastoral Symphony, 1922, considered V. W's best, still unrecorded).

English Folk Songs—Suite (collected by V. W. —orch. Jacob)—C. B. Symph. (Barlow) 2–10″ in Set cm–x159. See Liadov. For a sterner

Recommended Recordings

V. W. note the *Symphony in F Minor*, composed 1935 (VM–440).

VILLA-LOBOS, HECTOR (b. 1884)

A Festival of Brazilian Music—Brazilian Festival
Quartet & Orch. (Marx); Schola Cantorum
(Ross); Elsie Houston, soprano. 5–12″ in Set
VM–773. Album contains two major works of
V-L: *Bachiana Brasileira No. 1* (1932) and
Nonetto (1923) as well as two songs and the
subtle *Quartet for Harp, Celesta, Flute, Saxo-
phone and Women's Voices* (1931). See page
154. Note also the *Brazilian String Quartet*
(V–11212/3).

VIVALDI, ANTONIO (1678–1743)

Violin Concerto in D Major, Op. 3, No. 9—Jean
Fournier (violin) with harpsichord & orchestra. 12″ No. AS–37.—By the noted violinist-
composer who picked up the development of
the concerto where Corelli left off, placing in
his debt many of his contemporaries of whom
Sebastian Bach was one.

WAGNER, RICHARD (1813–1883)

*Prelude and Love-Death from Tristan and
Isolde* (1857–59)—Berlin Philharmonic (Furtwängler) 2–12″ in Set VM–653. From the same
work note *Love Duet* (Melchior; Leider; orch.
Coates, V–7523/4). See p. 66. In addition note,

Recommended Recordings

Prelude and Good Friday Spell from Parsifal
(1877–82)—Berlin Philharm. (Furtwängler)
3–12″ in Set VM–514.—F's playing of both the
Tristan and Parsifal excerpts is an experience
not to be missed. Note also *Wagnerian Excerpts* (Toscanini, VM–853) and *Magic Fire
Music from Die Walküre* (Stokowski, V–15800).

WALTON, WILLIAM T. (b. 1902)

Concerto for Viola and Orchestra (1928–29)—
Freder. Riddle & London Symph. (Walton)
3–12″ in Set D–8. See page 150.

Facade Suite No. 2 (1938)—London Philharm.
(Walton) 12″ No. V–12532 & Orch. Raymonde
(Goehr) 12″ No. C–69834D.—Consists of six
deftly sophisticated pieces. Also note W's
spirited march *Crown Imperial* (V–12031); the
satyrical *1st Facade* (V–12034/5); the 1934–35
Symphony (D–25600/5) awaited with such
eagerness it was snatched from the composer
and played in London before it was completed.
Also his *Violin Concerto* (VM–868).

WEBER, C. M. VON (1786–1826)

Der Freischutz (1820) Overture—London Philharm. (Beecham) 12″ No. C–68986D. See page
52. Note also *Overture to Oberon* (1826) 12″
No. C–69410D.

Index

[211]

Index

Index

Index

[214]

Index